DUKE ELLINGTON

Kent Smith

MELROSE SQUARE PUBLISHING COMPANY
LOS ANGELES, CALIFORNIA

Consulting Editors for Melrose Square
Raymond Friday Locke
Mitchell S. Burkhardt

Originally published by Melrose Square, Los Angeles.
©1992 by Kent Smith.

All rights reserved under International and Pan-American Copyright Conventions. No part of this book may be reproduced in any form or by electronic or mechanical means including information storage and retrieval systems without permission in writing from the publisher, except by a reviewer who may quote brief passages in a review. Published in the United States by Melrose Square Publishing Company, an imprint of Holloway House Publishing Company, 8060 Melrose Avenue, Los Angeles, California 90046. ©1992 by Kent Smith.

Cover Painting: Lam Triet
Cover Design: Bill Skurski

DUKE ELLINGTON

MELROSE SQUARE BLACK AMERICAN SERIES

ELLA FITZGERALD
singer
NAT TURNER
slave revolt leader
PAUL ROBESON
singer and actor
JACKIE ROBINSON
baseball great
LOUIS ARMSTRONG
musician
SCOTT JOPLIN
composer
MATTHEW HENSON
explorer
MALCOLM X
militant black leader
CHESTER HIMES
author
SOJOURNER TRUTH
antislavery activist
BILLIE HOLIDAY
singer
RICHARD WRIGHT
writer
ALTHEA GIBSON
tennis champion
JAMES BALDWIN
author
JESSE OWENS
olympics star
MARCUS GARVEY
black nationalist leader
SIDNEY POITIER
actor
WILMA RUDOLPH
track star
MUHAMMAD ALI
boxing champion
FREDERICK DOUGLASS
patriot & activist
MARTIN LUTHER KING, JR.
civil rights leader

CONTENTS

1
A Royal Evening   9

2
Not So Humble Beginnings   21

3
New York, New York   39

4
Gangsters to Royalty   59

5
Roaditis   87

6
The Rollercoaster of Success   105

7
Rebound   141

8
Ambassador of Music   159

9
Diminuendo   173

Chapter One

A Royal Evening

ON A QUIET SPRING evening in Washington D.C. in 1969, the President of the United States, Richard M. Nixon, hosted an unpresedented birthday party for a 70-year-old black man. It was in honor of his life-time contribution to music, an honor that had been late coming, but had finally arrived. His name was Duke Ellington and he was one of the giants of American Jazz music. He had proven his musical genius many times over, and was labled by many as the "Einstein of melody," for his prodigious and innovative musical creations.

Duke Ellington's music had been rediscovered and he was being hailed as a genius when President Richard M. Nixon honored him with a special White House dinner in the fall of 1969.

Earlier that evening, during a press conference, a reporter tried to get the Duke to comment on politics by asking him what he thought about the generation gap. Ellington refused to get into a political discussion, and replied, "I don't believe in the generation gap. I believe in regeneration gaps. Each day you regenerate, or else you're not living."

It wasn't an artful dodge; it was Ellington's nature. He was a man so in love with music that he couldn't let the daily problems of life interfere. It was no idle jest that he titled his autobiography "Music Is My Mistress," for it truly was. When it came to music, there was no racism, no politics. He hoped his music could heal what was being torn apart.

Even Nixon's guest list was surprisingly non-partisan, thoroughly integrated, and chock full of politically unusual characters. Benny Goodman, Count Basie, Cab Calloway, and Dizzy Gillespie mingled with Vice-President Spiro Agnew and Attorney General John Mitchell. Ministers of many religions and university presidents stood along side lawyers, top corporate executives, a famous Hollywood film director, and sundry jazz musicians: white, black, Hispanic.

Many members of Duke's immediate family were there. He escorted his sister, Ruth, who wore a daring blonde wig. His son, Mercer and his family, but Duke's legal wife, Edna, was not there, nor his lifelong mistress, Beatrice Ellis (Evie Ellington). His closest friends were naturally invited. His personal doctor and long-time friend, Arthur Logan; as well as Harry Carney; Tom Whaley; and his dear friends from England, Renee and Leslie Diamond; and Stanley Dance, the British music critic and Ellington chronicler.

In a politically turbulent decade, it was a remarkably non-political evening, and Ellington behaved well, as he always did, elegantly but with touch of benign levity, gracious to all but subservient to none.

In the receiving line, President Nixon observed that Ellington kissed each person four times no matter his or her rank, social standing fame or wealth. Finally he couldn't stand it any longer and blurted, "Why four kisses?"

"One for each cheek, Mr. President," Ellington said as simply and guilelessly as he always did.

Then, later, as Nixon presented him the Medal of Freedom, Ellington warmly gave him four kisses, two pecks on each cheek, and Nixon smiled back.

No woman, not even the First Lady, was

spared his charming flattery. At the dinner table, before the medal presentation, Pat Nixon mentioned that her daughter had seen Ellington earlier that day. "Oh, yes," he said, "and you have a beautiful daughter." Then he added. "Mrs. Nixon, have you heard of the White House Ordinance?"

"White House Ordinance?" she said, perplexed.

"Yes. There is a law that no First Lady can be prettier than a certain degree, and you are exceeding the legal limit."

The First Lady said, matching the Duke's jocular tone, "I've heard about *you*."

Duke's frivolity was deceptive. He was an indefatigable composer, band leader, and had spent 53 years touring the globe and playing his music virtually non-stop. There was his famous statement, when a columnist asked him if he was getting ready to retire: "Retire to what?"

An evening as the honored guest in an unprecedented White House birthday party was not an excuse to take a day off. By the next evening, he would be just as graceful and jocular with the cowboys in Oklahoma City as he had been with the President of the United States.

After receiving the Medal of Freedom from

Duke Ellington and President Richard M. Nixon in 1969 when Ellington was honored for his contribution to American music. Many great jazz names from his era were there.

The White House. President Richard M. Nixon hosted and unpresedented birthday party to mark Duke Ellington's 70th birthday and to laud his contribution to American music.

Among the guests were Benny Goodman, Count Basie, Cab Calloway and Dizzy Gillespie who mingled with the likes of Vice-President Spiro Agnew and Attorney General John Mitchell.

the President, Ellington was indeed touched. This was the culmination of a life. He'd gone from being a popcorn vendor in a Washington baseball park to receiving the highest civilian honor. He'd suffered racism and been shunned by both blacks and whites. Whites because he was black; blacks because they felt his music was too white. He made annual appearances at Carnegie Hall during the 40s, but still played in honky-tonks from Maine to California. He was the rave in England during the 30s and dined with the King of England in 1933. Yet, when he returned to New York, he couldn't even get a room at a mediocre uptown hotel.

His music spanned the entire history of jazz, directing, adapting, influencing the only pure musical art form to have come out of America. He'd received honors from France, Liberia, Sweden, and many other countries.

This was not Ellington's first encounter at the White House, or with a president. He'd been invited to play, for one reason or another, by several presidents. President Truman, wanting to converse as one piano player to another, had invited Ellington into his study, dismissed the guards, and acted like "a couple of cats in a billiard parlor," as Ellington described it.

The great Count Basie with Duke Ellington rehearsing at the "All Star Swing Festival" at Lincoln Center. The festival featured many of the stars of the Big Band era.

On another occasion, he bumped into Dwight Eisenhower in a hotel before an engagement at the White House, and Ike asked if Duke could please play "Mood Indigo." He did, four times during the evening. He'd been invited by President Lyndon Johnson seven times, twice to entertain, and the rest as a guest. He premiered his "The Liberian Suite" when Johnson had invited the President of the Republic of Liberia. By the end of the evening, Ellington was jamming with the Marine band. In his autobiography, he warmly recalls the evening, "I only wish I had a picture of Paul Gonsalves coming out the front door of the White House, weaving slightly, his horn in his hand, and just a little bombed."

It was indeed a profound honor to have President Nixon bestow upon him the highest civilian honor on his 70th birthday. So touched was Ellington that his thoughts turned back to the past as he said, "There's no place I would rather be tonight except in my mother's arms."

He had been very close to his mother, Daisy Kennedy Ellington, who had a great influence on his life, even after her death 35 five years previously.

Sentimentality, if it ever appeared at all, didn't last long with the Duke. His charm quickly returned, and soon the President himself was banging the piano keys, leading a cheery round of "Happy Birthday."

After Nixon's round of "Happy Birthday," the stage was given to the impressive collection of musicians, including guest pianists Dave Brubeck, Billy Taylor and the incredible Earl Hines, whose "Perdido" got the crowd roaring with appreciation. Ellington was especially touched when he saw his life-long friend and mentor, Willie "The Lion" Smith, banging on the President's concert grand, "...still with a derby on his head."

After an hour and a half, and past midnight, Nixon announced that the party would continue for the music lovers for as long as they wished.

Duke Ellington went directly to his hotel, changed from tux to his travel clothes, and departed for his plane without so much as ruffling the sheets on his bed.

Chapter Two

Not So Humble Beginnings

EDWARD KENNEDY "DUKE" ELLINGTON was born April 29th 1899 in a unique situation in Washington D.C. Although his parents, James Edward Ellington and his mother, Daisy Kennedy, were working-class, they were able to supply a surprisingly middle class environment for their new-born son to grow up in.

James Edward, called J.E. by his friends and son, originally worked as a butler, and was even occasionally employed at the White House. He eventually settled into a job at the Navy's blueprinting office, but still occasional-

---

Gertrude "Ma" Rainey was the first blues singer to become nationally known and was the first to make records. Her popularity was soon challenged by the talented Bessie Smith.

ly moonlighted as a butler and assisted various relatives in the catering business.

Daisy was the daughter of a Washington policeman, and had five brothers and five sisters. They were a close family, and Daisy, with her son in hand, would spend much time at her mother's house along with all those loving aunts surrounding the little boy. As Duke himself said, "I was pampered and pampered and spoiled rotten by all those women."

He was raised virtually as an only child. His sister, Ruth, the only other member of the family, wasn't born until 16 years later.

The relatives who were in the catering business, worked for some of the richest families in the Washington area, providing J.E. with employment opportunities.

Food and civility were never lacking in the Ellington house. J.E. passed on the same manners he learned as a butler to his son. They always has a properly set table, ate well, and lived a life style far surpassing the majority of blacks, and many whites, at the turn of the century, an era which did not bode well for blacks. It was still two decades before women would be given the right to vote, and although black men could vote, intense racism had excluded them from congress and the upper echelons of society. In fact, it wouldn't be until Duke was in his mid-sixties before the first black man would enter the congress since the decade following the Emancipation Proclamation.

Not only did his life span the entire history of jazz, he witnessed some of the most socially turbulent, racially chaotic changes in Western history. He was a young man when the Dough Boys were battling the Kaiser, and he was still composing music when Saigon fell to the North Vietnamese. He was born in a time when the best a black man could hope for in a political career was to be a butler in a senator's house; he died in a time when one was sitting on the Supreme Court.

For entertainment, youngsters of the time would read pulp westerns and detective stories, and Duke was no exception. He read voraciously, kept up on sports through the newspaper, and read the scandalous but thrilling stories in the "Police Gazette," and all the Sherlock Holmes stories he could get hold of.

For more illicit adventures, he used to sneak into pool halls. Between the games of pool, he met and developed relationships with some of the best musicians in the Washington area, who were some of the best in the country.

The ghetto was as alien to Duke as it was to any middle class child of the time, white or black. His father dressed well, and kept his son in fine clothing. J.E. always acted as if he were a millionaire, spoke impeccable English, and never passed up an opportunity to give a lady a compliment. Duke's charming flattery came from his father, who used to compliment a young lady by saying something a little off beat like, "Oh, you make that hat look beautiful."

As a child, the world of music and piano playing was far from him. His passion was baseball. He lived for the game, and engaged in other sporting activities as well, running, football, whatever he could do. He was quick, strong and fast. To stay in shape, he used to go on long walks all over the city with his cousin Sonny Ellington, visiting various relatives and getting a scrumptious meal at each stop. It was one of the advantages of having a lot of relatives in one city. Just about everywhere he went, he was welcomed.

It was an accident, literally, that got him into playing the piano. After getting hit in the head with a baseball bat, his mother was so concerned she made him take piano lessons in an effort to get him off the street and back inside where it was safe. In the beginning, he showed neither interest nor talent for the piano, preferring baseball to the keyboard.

Aside from sports, Duke also displayed a

President Theodore Roosevelt. Duke Ellington recalled that, when he was a child, the president would stop and watch him and his friends playing baseball near the White House.

natural talent for drawing and painting, much more than for music. But even this took a backseat to baseball. When Duke and his friends weren't hanging around the ball part, they would play ball in a tennis court not far from the White House. Several times, Duke recalled, President Theodore Roosevelt passed by riding his horse, paused and watched the children play for a few minutes, then waved to them as he left.

He eventually got a job at the stadium selling popcorn and hot dogs. It was the perfect summer job for a young baseball lover.

His next summer job was while he and his mother spent the summer at a seaside resort, Asbury Park, just before he entered high school. Because he looked older than he was, he was able to land employment as a dishwasher, but it didn't work out quite the way he expected. For one, the water was scalding hot and he wasn't very fast. A cook named Bowser, however, took a liking to Duke, and showed him such tricks as retrieving a plate from the bottom of the sink of scalding water with his bare hands. Bowser was also a fan of piano music, and told Duke to look up a guy named Harvey Brooks, who was playing down in Philadelphia. "He's your age," Bowser said. "You've got to hear him play.

He's terrific."

On his way back to Washington, Duke stopped by and listened to the teenager wildly banging on the keyboard. He had a wicked left hand and the music was exciting and compelling and different, but it wasn't jazz. At the time, the hot music was ragtime, fast paced boogie-woogie music that made the listener want to swing, clap and dance.

That evening was important because it changed Duke's attitude about the piano. Instead of an instrument of torture, as it had been, the piano was alive, fun, invigorating.

When he returned to Washington, he got a part time job behind the counter at a soda fountain. While stuck in the house one week with a cold, thinking about Harvey Brooks playing that inspiring ragtime, Duke started diddling with the piano and came up with his first musical creation, "Soda Fountain Rag." He played it around town and was surprised with the effect it had on people. They liked it.

Duke entered Armstrong High, an all-black school that specialized in teaching vocational skills. Coming from a practical family, Duke knew that many doors to success would be closed to him, so he wanted to use his education to his advantage. He knew that his best bet would be to acquire a skill, and he wanted

Washington, D. C. Born in Washington to a working-class couple whose large family was able to supply a comfortable environment to their son, Duke recalled later that he was

terribly spoiled as a child. Duke's mother had five younger sisters, all childless when he was born. "I was pampered and pampered and spoiled rotten by all those women," he said.

to develop his drawing talent as a vocation. He studied mechanical drawing and painting in hopes of becoming a commercial artist, and he showed great talent. He won a prestigious poster contest sponsored by the National Association for the Advancement of Colored People, which landed him a college scholarship in the arts, but he never took advantage of it. Something drastic would happen to Duke while in high school that would change his entire outlook on life, and it began when he met a boy named Edgar McEntree. McEntree was popular at parties, dressed very well, and knew his way around town, much like Ellington, who had taken to wearing a tie, shiny shoes, and fashionable suits. Ellington was tall, reeked with self confidence, and carried himself with an aristocratic manner. Still, McEntree felt that if Ellington was going to be his friend, he'd need some kind of title to make him "special." All McEntree's friends had to be special in some way, so he started calling his new friend "Duke," and the name stuck.

Impressed by Duke's sound, McEntree had him play at a senior party, although he was still a freshman. Duke had just composed another piano piece, "What Do You Do When The Bed Breaks Down," which he also played, and the crowd was ecstatic.

It was at that party that Duke finally got seriously interested in music, and lost his passion for athletics. It wasn't because the crowd loved it, or he felt he was talented, or some voice from the heavens told him it was his destiny. The next morning, three very pretty young ladies showed up at his house, and asked his father if they could escort Duke to school.

After turning the corner, they turned to him and asked him to skip school so they could go to another "hop" or dance party, where he could play more of his infectious music. It was the way his piano playing seemed to attract the ladies that caught Duke's interest, and he kept going to parties and continued playing.

Duke kept studying art, but his creative piano playing caught the attention of the high school music teacher, Henry Grant, who offered Duke private lessons. From Grant, Duke learned the formal side of music, theory and harmony, but it was in the pool halls that he learned that music has a soul all its own.

Frank Holliday's poolroom was one of Duke's favorite hangouts. An old beat up piano stood in the corner and musicians from all over would take turns banging on the keys. Duke would listen and listen to the various players, picking up tricks and technique. Some were trained at the conservatory, others couldn't even read music. But it didn't seem to matter, the atmosphere was relaxed and playful, and the formal players got along beautifully with those who played by ear, exchanging ideas and keyboarding tricks.

Although Duke wasn't in their league, they didn't seem to mind the upstart asking questions and trying out some of the bridges and tricky parts. It was there that Duke met "Doc" Perry, who, like Grant, befriended the promising and enthusiastic young man, and gave him his first solid grounding on the piano. He spent many hours with Duke during those years and never once did he ever ask for anything in return. To Perry, Duke's enthusiasm and love for music were enough.

It was during this experimental period that Duke started developing his own style. When he came across an interesting piece, but it proved too difficult for him to do, he would change it around a bit so he could play it, but still managed to retain the flavor, mood, and more importantly, imbuing the song with his personality.

Many of the parties that Duke attended were called "rent" parties. To attend, the guests paid a fee and bought their own drinks. The money basically went to pay the rent of the host, and maybe a little for the piano player.

At first, Duke attended the parties not as a piano player—he didn't know that many tunes. In fact, aside from the two he'd composed, he didn't know any. Louis Thomas, a ragtime pianist of some repute, offered to let Duke play for one of his gig bands. At the time, Thomas was also working as a booking agent, sending out other pianists and bands for occasions he couldn't make. He offered to let Duke play with his least accomplished players if he could learn "The Siren Song," which Duke did in a day. But the appointment was rather disappointing. Duke didn't know anything else, and just sat at the piano, listening to requests until someone pipped up with "The Siren Song." But that's all he knew, so he kept playing it over and over, changing the tempo, adding a few flourishes here and there, to make it sound different. While the crowd was pleased, Duke wasn't, and set to work learning other tunes. Soon, he was getting some pretty steady work. The strangest gig he played was for a magician who also told fortunes during his act. Duke was to accompany both the act and the fortune telling, setting different moods for the various tricks and effects, and this proved to be a bonus. Not only was he improvising, he learned to quickly adapt and fit a specific mood, and proved to be quite good at it.

On his time off, he would get with a few other musicians, Otto Hardwick on the saxophone, Arthur Whetsol on the trumpet, and banjo player Elmer Snowden, and attempt to imitate the sounds of other bands. Without knowing it, they were setting up the stage for the next big phase in Ellington's career, his first band.

It was while playing for Thomas that Duke realized that the money was in the booking, not the playing. He broke away, set up his own music agency, and was lining up gigs for five different bands. In addition, he also had a little sign painting business on the side. So he would paint the sign for a party, book the band, and show up to play the piano himself. He was making money on all sides, enough to build a ten-room house and buy a Cadillac before his 21st birthday. Not bad for any young man in 1918, and all that much more remarkable for a black youth.

In July of that same year, Duke married his childhood sweetheart, Edna Thompson. She grew up in the house across the street. They went to the same schools, had the same classes, and, in high-school, Edna was Duke's girl.

That year, Duke took on yet another job. He

During his formative years, Duke Ellington would play the background music for stage acts. While doing this, he grew proficient at improvising by setting the moods for each act.

worked at the State Department as part phone operator and part messenger. He would get a call from a military officer who would request tickets for a certain destination. Duke would then rush down to the train station, figure out which train the officer had to catch, buy the tickets, and then deliver them. Not only was he efficient, but he also learned all the major train schedules, which later helped him when he started touring his band around the country. In light of his successful band booking business, the extra job seemed superfluous, but the next year, the reason became obvious. Edna gave birth to a son, Mercer Kennedy Ellington.

Although the business was going well, Duke's passion continued to be with his music, and he started getting an itch for bigger and better things. But it wasn't until he happened to hear the incredible "Carolina Shout" by James P. Johnson that his imagination was completely captured.

So taken by "Carolina Shout," which Duke listened to over and over on his friend's player piano where he could slow the mechanism down and see how the notes were put together, he eventually learned it by heart, and played it at parties and around town.

Not long after, James P. Johnson came to

Washington for a concert. Duke's friends pushed him toward the stage and shouted, "He can play 'Carolina Shout' as good as the master!" James P. bowed out and let the young upstart take a turn at the piano. Duke, scared and nervous, performed with flair and style. So impressed was Johnson, he even applauded, and dubbed the Duke his personal guide after the concert to all the hot joints in town. It was the start of one of many friendships that, years later, would help the young Duke Ellington, through some hard times in New York.

While James P. Johnson's music had the invigorating tempo of ragtime, it was different, more soulful. It was totally new, and Duke wanted to be part of this new sound. It didn't have a name at the time, but it was catching on fast, as well as creating quite a stir among the more conservative, puritanical ranks of the country, who accused it of being vulgar, sexual, and decadent.

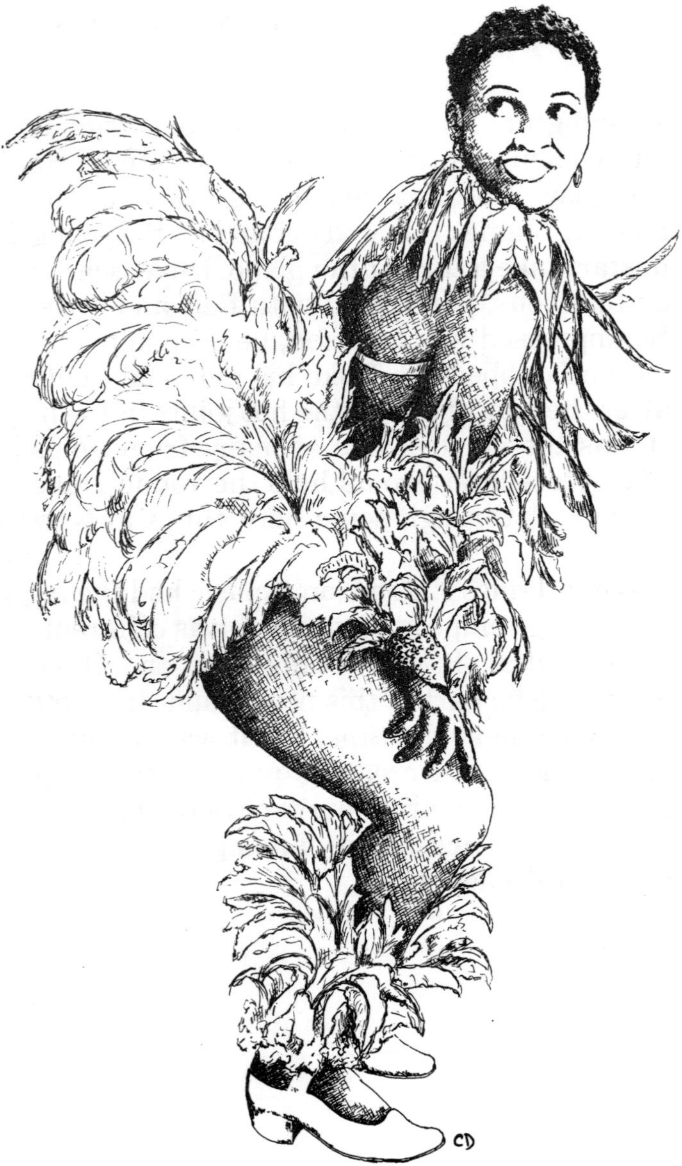
CD

―――― *Chapter Three* ――――

New York, New York

ALTHOUGH DUKE'S BUSINESS WAS booming in Washington, earning him nearly two hundred dollars a week (about $600 by today's standards), Duke was always excited when he talked with musicians from out of town—St. Louis, New Orleans, Chicago, Kansas City, but especially New York, where the center of the world was located. At least musically speaking.

In Washington D.C., Ellington was playing for largely white audiences and middle-class blacks, who where still shying away from the James P. Johnson style of music and the new

---

As far as many were concerned, New York was the Cotton Club with it's elaborately costumed showgirls. It was the place every band wanted to play, including Duke Ellington's.

"vulgar" sound. The type of music he usually played was foxtrots, waltzes, ballads, and ragtime. Years later, as Duke became a top jazz composer, he incorporated much of what he learned from white music, blending the two forms into his unique and elegant style.

On his time off, however, it was down to the pool halls and smoke-filled bars where he could meet with musicians from all over the east, and jam together in a relaxed atmosphere. One such musician was a flashy young New Jersey drummer who had had the fortune to have worked in Harlem. His name was Sonny Greer, and he had just finished a job as a drummer in a trio with Fats Waller in Ashbury Park before moving to Washington. Greer just happened to be shooting some pool in a hall next to the Howard Theater when a sudden need for a drummer came up. The show was due to start in 30 minutes. Greer nonchalantly, with a touch of arrogance, volunteered for the job. He proved to be as good as he boasted.

While at the Howard, he struck up an acquaintance with Otto "Toby" Hardwick, one of Ellington's closest friends. He grew up less than a block from Duke's home. Duke took a liking to this very tiny person, who was five years his junior, and a fan of both baseball and music. He looked after the young man, and persuaded him to switch from base fiddle, which his father had to carry to school and work for him because he was too small to lift it, to the C-melody saxophone. After quickly mastering the horn, Duke sent the youngster out on jobs, and he soon developed quite a reputation as a sax player.

Through Hardwick, Ellington soon met Greer and they instantly got along. "There was some sort of magnetism to him you wouldn't understand," Greer later said about his first impression of Duke Ellington. "In my whole life, I've never seen another man like him. He walks into a strange room, and the whole place lights up."

Duke was impressed with Greer as well, but more because he had been in New York. Duke and other members of his band waited to talk to Greer after a show, just to see if he was as cool as he appeared. "He answered our questions with a line of jive that laid us low," Duke said in his autobiography about the incident. It wasn't long after that Greer quit the Howard, and joined Duke's band.

In addition to Greer and Hardwick, the core players of Ellington's first band was formed. Arthur Whetsol was the trumpeter and Elmer Snowden handled the banjo.

Greer ignited the group with his wild tales

Ellington, seated at the piano, and "The Washingtonians" in 1925, after they moved to New York and found acceptance with the audiences at the Kentucky Club. Standing behind Ellington is

saxophonist Otto "Toby" Hardwick. He and drummer Sonny Greer joined Ellington at the beginning and would remain for several decades, although the relationships were stormy at times.

of life in New York, of the glamorous clubs and personalities to be found up there. Greer also added a lot of flash and tricks to their playing style, to make it more invigorating with the audience. Like Duke, he exuded self-confidence, but it was Ellington who added the elegance to their playing.

For a while, they lived it up. After playing a paying gig, even though it was late, they'd head out for other clubs, to which they often raced other musicians in their big new cars. After 1920, the late night clubs were often illicit speakeasies, where they could mess around with other musicians, have fun, play their own music, smoke big fat cigars, drink whisky or gin, and pretend they were living the good life of the big city.

It is little wonder why Duke, in 1922, suddenly left his lucrative band booking and sign painting business to move to New York when he got a job offer. Wilbur Sweatman, noted for playing three clarinets at the same time, had contacted Sonny Greer about doing some accompaniment for his vaudeville act, then the hottest thing going in show business. Greer agreed, provided there was also work for all five, and Sweatman agreed in principle, but found work only for Ellington, Greer and Hardwick. Snowden and Whetsol were on their own. Duke said he didn't get much musical satisfaction from working in vaudeville, but he picked up a lot about show business. Vaudeville was a live variety show. Singers, dancers, comedy acts, animal tricks, jugglers, and spectacular acrobats would follow one after another. The band would warm up the crowd before the show, accompany the different acts, and play after, as the audience was letting out.

Within a few weeks, however, Sweatman's gigs cooled off, and Greer, Ellington and Hardwick were on their own, scrounging around for food money, playing for tips and hustling in the pool halls. Greer was quite a pool player. He would start off with a quarter, and when he had run it up to two bucks, he'd quit, and they'd go out for a steak dinner, give the waitress a quarter tip, and have another quarter left to start over the next day.

It was during this period that Ellington developed his friendship with Willie "The Lion" Smith and James P. Johnson. The Lion would let Ellington play with him, and split tips. He was always encouraging him, and helped out from time to time.

Duke also found inspiration in the Broadway movie houses. It was the days of silent movies, and a symphony orchestra would play along with the film, performing various classical pieces. "If there was a good Western on you'd probably sit through three performances of a symphony," Duke remembered later.

While life was hard, it wasn't desperate. The stories of splitting a hotdog five ways, Duke later admitted, were more of a gag than the truth. There was a wealth of clubs, especially the speakeasies, and rent parties to play at, and the pool halls, but they were getting tired of the lifestyle more than anything, and he was tired of just listening.

One day Duke found fifteen dollars in the street; he bought the group a meal and tickets back to Washington.

They tried again in the spring of the following year, 1923. Greer's friend, Fats Waller, came to Washington to play at a burlesque show. Ellington had gotten to know him while he was in New York so naturally he visited his friend. Waller told Ellington that he was quitting his New York job the next week, and he and Greer should take it over. He assured them that there would be work for Hardwick, Snowden and Whetsol.

Enthused with the prospects of a steady job in New York, they all jumped at the chance. Duke had saved up a little money, and sent the group up ahead of him, to get things arranged. When they arrived, however, Greer and the others found that Waller had just left without arranging a replacement.

Thinking that the job was secure, Ellington traveled lavishly, eating quite well and riding first class all the way. He was shocked to discover that the other four were broke and had been waiting for Ellington to bail them out.

There was a big difference between this trip and the one the previous year. They'd been playing as a band in Washington, and started developing a strong camaraderie, and were dedicated to keeping the band together. Willie "The Lion" Smith was there, once again, when Ellington needed him, and so was a guitarist they'd gotten to know, Freddy Guy. Both of them would let Ellington sit in during a gig, and they'd split tips to help him out.

They happened to meet up with a nightclub singer, Ada Smith (nicknamed "Bricktop" because of her short red hair), who had listened to them in Washington and was impressed. She was able to persuade the owner of a night club, Barron Wilkins, to make these Washingtonians his house band. Barron's was a popular night club with successful black, and occasionally white entertainers, such as Al Jolson, dropping by.

While they didn't play anything particularly innovative or sensational, the band had showmanship.

At the time, Elmer Snowden was actually the band's leader. He handled all the business arrangements and payed the members. With the simple steady work, it was not a hard task. Duke Ellington was the pianist and inspiration for much of their original music. He had begun to imitate James P. Johnson and The Lion's striding technique, and was starting to lean to a more jazz sound in the playing, but basically, the music was straight and conventional.

Duke teamed up with Joe Trent, and peddled a few songs around, but didn't get any bites until they played a song for Fred Fisher, a songwriter himself and the man who wrote "Chicago."

After listening to their song, Fisher said, "I like it."

"We'd like a fifty dollar advance," Joe said.

"Okay. Give me a lead sheet and I'll sign the contract," Fisher said.

"Give the man a lead sheet," Joe said turning to Duke.

The problem was that Duke had never written a lead sheet, or tried to write down his music at all. In Washington, he'd had others

Fats Waller was already a big star when Ellington and the Washingtonians moved to New York. He quickly became a fan and recommended Ellington to several club owners.

do it for him, for copyright reasons, but never on his down. It was 4:30 p.m., and the office closed at five. So Duke set to work in a room filled with ten pianos, all banging away, and crudely worked out a lead sheet.

They didn't get any breaks for a while, but one day Joe caught Duke on Broadway and said he had something. It was a musical but they had to write it that night. Duke, not knowing any better, not realizing that composers usually spent months writing an entire show, said, "Okay," and set to work. By the next day they demonstrated the show for Jack Robbins, and he loved it. They asked for a five hundred dollar advance, and Robbins pawned his wife's engagement ring to give it to them. As it turned out, it was a fantastic investment. Robbins took the show to Germany, where it ran for two years at the Berlin Wintergarten.

By autumn, the Duke and the Washingtonians were quite popular. They soon quit Barron's and moved uptown to the Hollywood Club (later renamed as the Kentucky Club).

With the move, the structure of the band changed drastically. Elmer Snowden, being successful with other business ventures, quit the band, and was replaced with Freddy Guy, the guitarist who'd helped them out earlier in the spring. With Snowden gone, they needed someone to handle the finances, and they all agreed on Duke, who had good business sense. With Duke handling the finances and the songwriting, he naturally grew to be the band's leader.

The Kentucky Club was a lucky break for an up-and-coming band. The audience was very uptown—classy socialites and celebrities. Jimmy Durante and Al Jolson were regulars. The environment was loose and free, and there was plenty of bootleg booze to go around. Gangsters supplying the illicit beverage were customers as well, mixing with the rich folk and famous movie stars. They were all big tippers and loved the music. But, as Duke later said, "We might leave with a hundred dollars in our pockets, but we'd blow it all going from joint to joint, finding out what was happening."

When the Kentucky closed, Duke and his friends would head to other clubs and parties, living it up the whole night. There were even breakfast dances in Harlem.

The wild, romantic lifestyle put a heavy strain on Duke's marriage—and his wife, Edna. They had left their son, Mercer, in Washington when they moved to New York. She was one of the show girls. She would walk out on stage in a provocative outfit, dance and lend a sensual atmosphere to the band, but otherwise, she had no real duties with the band. She had a hard time sharing her man with the public. Duke was widely loved and adored by everyone, including the young ladies—especially the young ladies. Rex Steward, a writer/musician who spent some years in the Ellington band, said, "Many of the lovely ladies upon whom Duke heaped exquisite compliments have succumbed. The number of his conquests is uncountable." Duke enjoyed the company of women, especially pretty ones. It was only a matter of time before a big blowup would happen. Finally, one of his affairs got out of hand, and he stayed away from home for three days. When he returned, Edna was in a rage. As Mercer Ellington, Duke's son, recounts the incident, "...he and mother got into a tremendous fight, in the course of which she got hold of his knife and slashed him across the face." For the rest of his life, Ellington never admitted how he got the scar on his face, and would get upset with anyone who asked, including reporters. Finally, the marriage crumbled, and Edna moved back to Washington with her son while Duke continued to play his music. Although their marriage didn't work out, Duke never divorced Edna and kept her in style for the rest of his life.

The stint at the Kentucky was a great period for experimentation, and the Ellington sound started changing from sweet society music, which was often played low so the audience could carry on a conversation, to more of a jazz sound.

He picked up a couple new band members, but instead of finding musicians to fit in with the "sweet" music, he hired those who played a more "jungle-istic" (Ellington's term) sound. Charlie "The Plug" Irvis, James "Bubber" Miley, Joe "Tricky Sam" Nanton were all renowned for putting mutes (either bent up tomato cans or rubber plungers) into the bell of their horns and making animal-like growling sounds. Irvis used to point his trombone right into the audience and growl. The technique came from New Orleans. Joe "King" Oliver occasionally used one in his trumpet, and Sidney Bechet, also from New Orleans, put one on his soprano saxophone.

Bubber Miley replaced Arthur Whetsol when he quit to go to medical school, and Nanton replaced Irvis. Miley and Nanton refined the growling tones, changing them from tricks into serious sound that both intrigued and stimulated the listeners. It was such a unique sound that Ellington gave up on "sweet" music altogether, and went with this new, raw jungle music. This was the start of his creative period, which lasted through every decade right into the 70s. By now, instead of borrowing and copying and adjusting the sounds of others, he was starting to lead with new, creative, intriguing and highly original music.

The Washingtonians caught the attention of Paul Whiteman, who, at the time, was billed as the "King of Jazz." Whiteman commissioned Duke to write a concert for his orchestra, which became "Blue Belles of Harlem."

Duke also met Irving Mills, a manger who was noted for picking up blues compositions from needy musicians at twenty dollars. The musicians often would turn the same number around and sell it again to Mills, but the joke was on them in the end. When Mills started recording some of those "ordinary" blues songs, he made a bundle. Years later when Mills was a recording success, Cootie Williams went to him to sell a piece and Mills asked him what it was.

"Just a blues song," Cootie said.

"Oh, no," Mills said getting animated. "I already own all the blues!"

It was through Mills that Duke started recording. After a few attempts, Duke soon learned how to adjust his playing to make it

Sheet music of an Ellington original composition. Millions of copies of dozens of these issues were sold—all produced by Mills Music. Owner Irving Mills was Ellington's manager.

sound better on the records, which had a tremendous amount of hiss and couldn't reproduce all the frequencies. What worked live didn't necessarily translate to the record. Always a master at adapting to a new form, Duke pushed certain parts and pulled back here and there to get a sound that would play better on a record, and soon became an expert recording artist. He recorded so much, for so many different labels, he had to use different names for the band: the Jungle Band, the Washingtonians, the Whoopee Makers, the Harlem Footwarmers.

Between his runs at the Kentucky Club, Duke would go on short tours, booked by Mills. It was a chance to get out of town and hear what people were doing outside of New York. He also found touring to be inspirational, even simple things like the color of the hills while the train passed through the countryside. A simple sign that said LEWANDO CLEANERS caught Duke's attention, and every time they passed it, they'd play around with a melody of the name. That lick grew into "East St. Louis Toodle-oo." It was a song that tried to paint a simple picture, as Duke once told Stanley Dance, "[It was] the broken walk of a man who had worked all day in the sun and was leaving the field at sunset."

It was during one of his summer New England tours that Duke offered Harry Carney, a teenage clarinetist, a job. Carney and his buddy, Johnny Hodges (saxophone), both inspired by Sidney Bechet, moved to New York from Boston to get into the music world. They landed jobs with Chick Webb, the drummer and band leader who gave Ella Fitzgerald her big break in show biz. Duke heard them play, and offered Carney a position that summer in New England. When the gig was over, Ellington was so impressed with the boy, he talked his mother into letting him move to New York instead of returning to school so he could be a permanent member of the band. She agreed and Duke became his guardian, and Carney was one of the few musicians who stuck with Ellington right up to the end, including several down periods when it looked as if Ellington's career had come to a dead end. He admired Duke so much that he said later, "It's not only been an education being with him, but also a great pleasure. At times I've been ashamed to take the money."

Carney also persuaded Duke to hire in his friend, Johnny Hodges, also a virtual life-long member of Ellington's band and later acclaimed as one of the jazz giants on the sax.

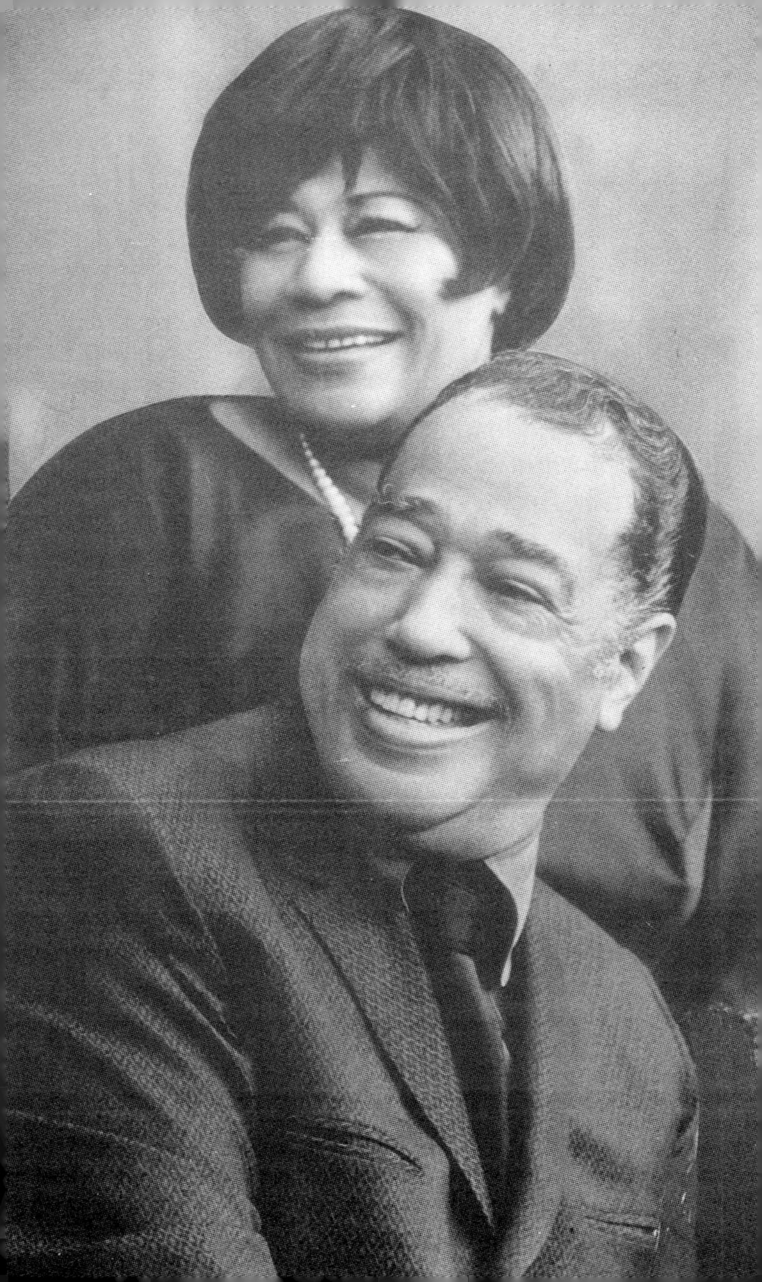

Chapter Four

Gangsters to Royalty

DUKE'S INTERNATIONAL acclaim started with a phone call from Irving Mills. Their run at the Kentucky Club had ended; it was back to one-night stands and weekend engagements out of town. The plan, at the time, was to get into the lucrative ballroom circuit, but the future was hazy. Duke was down in Philadelphia accompanying a vaudeville show when Mills called and said he'd lined up an audition for the Cotton Club.

This was 1927, the height of the roaring twenties, gangsters, crooked politicians, prohibition and bootlegging. It was a new era,

Ellington and Ella Fitzgerald first worked together in the 1930s and would often get back together for a tour, although he worked with other singers and she with other bands over the years.

wild and hectic. Girls cut their hair short. The Charleston was the dance craze. The country was on an economic roll. Nothing seemed to go wrong, and everyone wanted to celebrate. And jazz, with its bubbly tempo and quick appeal to the emotions, was their music. In just a few years it had gone from being the vulgar, uncultured sounds of the underprivileged to "the" music of the decade.

The Cotton Club was one of the top spots where it all happened: notorious gangsters, pretty showgirls, the social elite, and celebrities frequented the club. Although it was in Harlem, its clientele was mainly white. A few rich blacks got in, but for the most part, the people from the neighborhood never saw the inside of the Cotton Club unless they worked there as waiters, bus boys, dishwashers, cooks, or entertainers.

The previous band had been from the New Orleans/Chicago tradition, the most popular form of jazz at the time, and they were looking for a similar sound. They made an offer to Joe "King" Oliver himself. He was interested, but turned down the club's first offer for a long term run. He was holding out for more money, and felt he could get it.

Rather than barter, the owners of the Cotton Club decided to check out other bands, and have them come in to audition, and Mills happened to hear about it, virtually at the last minute, then made the hasty call to Duke.

The catch was that they were looking for an eleven-piece orchestra, and Duke was playing with six, sometimes seven. At first, the other band members didn't want to change the balance. Sonny Greer recalled, "That was one of the few times in my life I wanted to leave the band...to enlarge the band broke my heart because everything had been so quiet and tasteful."

Duke set to work hiring more musicians to make eleven, and arrived at the Cotton Club more than two hours late, but, as luck would have it, so did the managing owner, Harry Block. Duke's band was the first and only one he heard, and he offered them the job on the spot. "It was a classic example of being in the right place at the right time with the right thing before the right people," Duke later said about the incident.

There was one other problem, however. The engagement at the Cotton Club had been heavily advertised to begin on December 4, 1927, but Ellington had a contract to play through December 11 in Philadelphia, and the theater manager refused let him out of it.

Duke mentioned the dilemma to the people

New York's Cotton Club, the 1930s. It was "the place to be seen" but most of the people who were seen there in the audience were white. While all the entertainers were black, only

a few favored, famous and/or rich blacks were welcomed as customers. Duke Ellington played there first on December 4, 1927. In comparison to other bands his was sophisticated.

at the Cotton Club, and one of the proprietors knew a certain man in Philadelphia who commanded a certain amount of respect. He, in turn, sent one of his employees over to discuss the issue with the theater manager, and he had a sudden change of mind. Duke opened in the Cotton Club as billed.

The world of big show business was new to Ellington. He had been content with his small band, playing clubs and ballrooms, recording dates, and writing songs, but the Cotton Club was a whole new world. The music was written by Jimmy McHugh, the man who really pushed to get Ellington's band in the club. The club was owned by a group mainly out of Chicago, who, at first, resisted hiring an eastern band, preferring the sound from Chicago, where Joe "King" Oliver had been dominate for the past six years.

Band leaders of the time were usually very flashy, wearing provocative hats and wildly waving a baton. Duke suddenly found himself out of his league; he did none of those things, but never backed off from a good challenge. Their opening night at the Cotton Club didn't go well. They had traveled to New York the same day, and had rehearsed when they had a few free moments in Philadelphia with music sent down to them.

By the second night, the band settled down and started displaying some of their unique gifts. Duke was already a perfectionist. Now it was beyond perfection. He experimented with screens to place distinct shadows over parts of the band, or sometimes, he'd place the band behind a transparent curtain, creating a silhouette effect. One trumpeter, Freddy Jenkins, had had an accident when he was young resulting in the loss of the tips of his fingers of the right hand, his playing hand. Soon after joining Duke's orchestra, he was fingering his trumpet with the left. "With Duke," Jenkins later commented, "you're there to perform. You don't want them feeling sorry for you. You want them to enjoy the music."

Sonny Greer, in keeping with the elegant appearance, bought a brand new drum set costing over three thousand dollars—very lavish for the time. He also had Duke and his monogram on front of the bass drum. "I was the first in the world to do that," Sonny said in his autobiography.

The high standards didn't only apply to the entertainers, but the audience as well. Only the best dressed and groomed were allowed into the club, and even then, unless one was a recognizable celebrity or a regular, it took a heavy tip to the doorman to get in. During the floor show, no audience disturbance was tolerated. If a guest was talking too loudly, a waiter would politely ask him to quiet down. If he didn't, the captain would remind the rude person that he'd been cautioned. If he (or she) didn't behave, they'd be thrown out.

Everyone knew that bootlegged whisky was being sold at the Cotton Club, and just about any other club in the city, but its clientele was so prestigious that it had become off limits to the police, so long as the illicit sales were discreet. The usual whisky purchased at the time was called "Chicken Cock," and it was a bottle that came in a sealed can.

While the police weren't interested in the whisky, they were interested in solving other cases, many of which were connected with some of the gangsters who hung out in the clubs. "Every few weeks the homicide squad would send for me to go downtown," Duke reminisced later. "'Hey, Duke, you didn't know so-and-so, did you?' they would ask. 'No,' I'd say. But I knew all of them, because a lot of them used to hang out at the Kentucky Club, and things started really happening when we moved to the Cotton Club. But it wasn't healthy in those days to know very much."

Although Duke never mentioned who he

knew personally among the notorious gangsters, there are a couple of incidents where Al Capone came to his rescue. Someone discovered that some hoods were plotting to kidnap Duke and the famous dancer, Bill "Bojangles" Robinson, and hold them for ransom. Capone sent a few of his body guards to warn off the kidnappers at gun point

Another incident involved a road trip to Chicago. Some local thugs, after seeing Duke's name go up on a theater's marquee, demanded $500 for protection. Duke's road manager boasted that they didn't need any because the band members carried guns (which they didn't), and were crazy enough to get into a shoot out if the gangsters wanted. The road manager then brought up the incident with Duke, and he thought about moving the band out of town, but the hoodlums called up again, and demanded $200 this time. Duke rang up some connections, and soon Al Capone let the word out that Duke Ellington was to be left alone.

The biggest bonus that came with the Cotton Club engagement was the radio broadcasts. Radio was still a fairly new invention. In 1916 the first station went up and more quickly followed, but in the late 20s it was still a young medium and there was a lot of experimentation going on. Irving Mills, Duke's manager, cooked up a deal to broadcast the band from 6 to 7 every evening nationally. It was so popular that a transatlantic connection was arranged and soon Duke's music was being heard all the way to Europe where, unknown to him, jazz was becoming a sensation.

The years at the Cotton Club were also one of Duke's most richly experimental. He would switch parts that usually went to a clarinet player, for example, and give it to a trumpet. When a popular clarinetist from New Orleans, Barney Bigard, a legendary musician in his own right, joined the band, he was totally confused. "I used to think everything was wrong because he [Duke] wrote so weird. He would give someone else the part he should have given the clarinet player."

Freddy Jenkins described how Duke would arrive at some of his strange new sounds. He would pay his musicians union scale to just sit and play notes for him. They would start with a standard chord, then Duke would tell the trumpet and clarinet to switch notes. While it was the same chord, the quality would change. Duke would switch things around until he heard something he liked, then he'd work a new number around the sounds he'd created.

The Big Bands—Duke Ellington, Cab Calloway, Benny Goodman, the Dorsey brothers, issued in the "swing era" in nightclubs that featured a dance called "the jitterbug."

Some effects he discovered by accident. During the recording of "Black and Tan Fantasy" he noticed that the growl trombone and the growl trumpet were creating overtones through the mike, or mike tone. Rather then get rid of it, he started playing with the distance the instruments were from the mike, and changing the harmonics a bit to create the illusion of another instrument. The combination of the clarinet, trumpet and trombone in "Mood Indigo" is an excellent example of this new sound. Another time he was in Chicago doing a recording for RCA. He had the engineers move the mike around until he got just the right resonance, but it wasn't until they ended up in the men's room that Duke was pleased.

Unlike other composers, Duke often listened to the various improvisations of his band members, and when he heard something he liked, he'd work it into a melody, but not always for the instrument he first heard it on. Such switching often baffled the band members until they heard it performed. Cootie Williams later said about the early years with Duke, "In the beginning you didn't think about money. It was exciting. Everybody made suggestions. It was a family thing." Although Duke always had the last word, he gave a lot of credit and respect to his musicians.

In "Creole Love Call" he had singer Adelaide Hall lend some wordless vocals to the arrangement, which was probably the first time it had been done on a record.

With the larger band, it became necessary to start putting a lot of his arrangements down on paper, and they naturally grew in complexity. More than the experimental new sounds, the biggest improvement in Duke's writing was in his arrangements. Previously, with a band of only five, most of the numbers were written around the incredible Bubber Miley. Later, when Miley left due to illness (he later died in 1932), Cootie Williams, another Chick Webb player Duke lured into his camp, continued the tradition, even though he'd never used a mute before joining up with Duke. Realizing that Duke liked this new device, he started working with it himself, making the sound his own, a reflection of his own personality, not simply copying what Miley had done.

Over the next few years, other hits came out of the process, "Black and Tan Fantasy," "The Mooch," "Awful Sad," but the giant tune and Duke's first really big hit was "Mood Indigo," the number that President Eisenhower requested two and a half decades later.

He usually wrote the songs quickly, often at

the last minute. The evening before he was to record six tunes, he still had three yet to write. In fifteen minutes he had "Mood Indigo" worked out. The next evening, during the radio portion of the show, Duke played it, and the next day they were flooded with fan mail. It was an instant success. He and Irving Mills added some lyrics to it, and forty years later, royalties were still coming in.

He wrote "Black and Tan Fantasy" in the taxi on the way to a recording studio after staying up all night drinking at after hours clubs. In his autobiography he said he wrote "Solitude" while waiting for a session in Chicago because the previous band had gone over time. He leaned up against the glass, and scratched it out in 20 minutes, and after the band had played it, in Duke's own words, "I noted that everybody in the studio was moved emotionally. Even the engineer had a tear in his eye."

"What's it called?" the engineer asked.

"Solitude," Artie Whetsol replied.

Much of the motivation for recording original music came from Irving Mills. They'd started at the Cotton Club playing music from other composers, but Mills kept pushing for original work, especially when they went into the recording studio. As the tunes became popular, Duke naturally played them at the club between the shows and during the radio broadcasts, which, in turn, helped sell the records even more. Aside from the commercial benefits, it also escalated Duke's reputation as a composer.

Mills had been a singer before getting into management and music publishing. He was short, stocky, competitive, argumentative, fast-talking, and enjoyed waving his cigar wildly around while making a sales pitch: the epitome of the stereotypic agent. It was Mills' energy that broke new ground. For one, he was able to get Ellington records into previously white-only catalogs. He lined up a deal to be in a Hollywood movie, "Check and Double Check," featuring Amos 'n' Andy. A short film called "Black and Tan Fantasy" had been made of the band, much in the vein of an MTV style video, and a longer film, "Ring Dem Bells" was a big Ellington feature. Mills got Ellington's band in Florenz Ziegfeld's "Show Girl" (music by George Gershwin), and into the RKO Palace.

In addition to the bookings, Mills helped polish a number of Duke's lyrics, and was co-credited with such songs as "Sophisticated Lady," "Solitude," "Ring Dem Bells," "Caravan," and "Prelude to a Kiss."

Ivie Anderson, Duke Ellington, and Ella Fitzgerald in the late 1930s. Duke was at the height of what is sometimes referred to as his "first career," while Ella was on her way to becoming

one of the top jazz singers in the country. Ivie, the first woman to sing with Duke's band, was nearing the end of her long career. Herb Jeffries and Dorothy Dandridge replaced her.

By 1931, Duke's tenure at the Cotton Club had come to an end. Near the end of 1929, the great crash had taken place, and the wild, roaring lifestyle had come to a grinding halt. The good life was over. Those who'd been rich, were now dirt poor or, in some cases, suicides. Many of the gangsters were still around, but the night life had taken a sudden down swing.

Duke had always enjoyed the lifestyle of a traveling musician, and he decided to strike out across the country. Even though the country's economy was in shambles, the entertainment business was still fairly lucrative, but he had to go to where the money was because it was no longer coming to Harlem.

Unfortunately, being black in the United States in the 30s presented many problems. In the South, there were racial laws forbidding the bands to eat and sleep in hotels. Sometimes there simply was not enough time to find a suitable restaurant in the black area of town and return to the concert or dance hall in a white neighborhood. They often arrived, tired and hungry, and unable to purchase any food, sometimes from the very place they were playing!

In the North, local tradition and custom resulted in the same thing. A black person often risked humiliation if he or she haphazardly walked into the wrong restaurant.

Life on the road was not easy. There were no air conditioned buses or trains.

After one cross-country tour, and returning to New York city to be the first black band to play in the renowned Paramount Theater, Duke decided to rent two Pullman cars for just the band. They then would not have to worry about sitting in the right section on the train. When they arrived in a town, the Pullman's could be hooked up to electricity, water and sanitation facilities. There was a kitchen on board. His reputation with the railroad help was quite strong, and there was no lack for a helping hand from cooks and waiters.

During the early 30s, the band was enlarged to three trombonists and included a semi-permanent singer, Ivie Anderson. Although many others sang with Duke, including Lena Horne and Ella Fitzgerald, Ivie Anderson was always considered the best, the one who most closely matched Ellington's unique sound.

While Duke was popular in the states, he still suffered extreme racial prejudice from the critics, most of whom refused even to acknowledge Duke's music as an art form. Once a white cop stopped Duke and told him how much he liked his music. "If you were white, you'd be a great composer," the cop said sincerely.

Although he was breaking through some of the barriers, there were still an enormous amount left to crack; jazz was still not being taken seriously by American critics, despite its growing popularity, particularly among other musicians.

Europe, on the other hand, was a whole different affair. Without a tradition of intense racial prejudice, blacks were more quickly accepted, and jazz was creating quite a sensation.

The first to get a glimpse of this was Otto Hardwick. In 1929 he took leave of the Duke's band to do some traveling, and ended up for a while in Paris. He played at Ada "Bricktop" Smith's club for a while—the same "Bricktop" who helped book Duke Ellington at the Kentucky Club. Hardwick had also been well received in London.

When he returned, he described the unusually warm reception he got overseas, the popularity of jazz and especially Duke's music. Those transatlantic broadcasts had been paying off. Most members of the band thought Hardwick was exaggerating. After all, if it had been so great, why did he return to America?

Irving Mills, however, listened. He sensed something big might be in the wind. If even a fraction of what Hardwick said was true, there might be a tour in it. He started writing letters and pestering booking agencies and concert halls in Europe, trying to line up a tour for Duke Ellington.

In 1933 he finally succeeded, getting a date at the London Palladium, the most prestigious variety theater in the world.

Duke had been reluctant at first to travel overseas, not because he didn't believe his friend Hardwick; he was afraid of boats. When his mother had been pregnant with him, she was in a ferry boat that sunk. Duke listened many times to her retell the details of her rescue. Then, when he was a boy, he read about the sinking of the Titanic, and it fueled his phobia all that much more. The band members always joked that Ellington wouldn't even take the Hoboken ferry during their run at the Cotton Club. While steaming across the Atlantic, Duke was told that during the night, the ship was stirred by automatic pilot. "I don't understand how an automatic pilot can see an iceberg," Duke replied. It upset him so much, he would sit up the entire night watching for icebergs. He tried to get as many fellow band members as he could to help him, but usually they started falling off around three or four, and by five in the morning, everyone except

Duke would be quietly dreaming.

When he arrived in England, they knew right from the docks that they were in a different world. A group had gathered, and warmly greeted Duke and his jazz band, and followed them to their hotel. When Duke started talking to the press and music critics, he was astonished as to how well informed they were. They asked about music Duke had long forgotten, and more than once found himself unable to answer a question about his own music. Unfortunately, this also led to some problems during his tour. Fans often requested old Ellington hits, but Duke was more interested in playing his newer pieces.

The performance at the Palladium created quite a stir. The day after, an array of mixed reviews that hit the press, some praising Duke and others bashing him. But it was a "major" event in England at the time. It was being "written" about in the top papers of England, and Ellington was compared to Chopin, Debussy, Stravinsky, and others. It was quite a change from the press in the United States, where Ellington had been rather obscure for years while his popularity in Europe mushroomed. In 1928, when Stravinsky went to New York, he was asked by his American hosts what he wanted most to see. His answer,

"The Cotton Club." At the time, none of his American hosts had even heard of the club nor of Duke Ellington.

After the Palladium performance, Lord Beaverbrook, a newspaper tycoon, tossed a party in honor of Duke Ellington and his band. Two of Duke's most fervent fans were Prince George, the Duke of Kent, (killed during WWII) and the Prince of Wales (later the Duke of Windsor). At first, Duke didn't know who either of them were, and when Prince George requested "Swampy River," he got the brush off. Later, Duke said, that he and Prince George played a number of four hand duets, and the prince was a pretty good pianist.

The Prince of Wales was a drummer. He went over to Sonny Greer's set, and sat down Indian legged for the entire evening. As the evening wore on and the party goers consuming large quantities of gin, the young prince took a turn on Sonny's drums and banged out an impressive Charleston beat. The prince called him "Sonny," and Greer called him "The Wale." When "The Wale" introduced Ellington, he was presented as "The Duke of Hot."

Although the public had been greatly pleased, professional musicians and leading critics were disappointed. Spike Hughs, who had been instrumental in popularizing Ellington with British fans, was so disappointed he arranged with "Melody Maker," a jazz review magazine years ahead of America's "Down Beat," for a special performance for professional musicians—something that didn't cater to the easily titillated general public. Duke more than met the challenge, and unloaded his best shot and rifled the audience with jazz unlike they'd ever heard before. The British writer, Stanley Dance, who later co-authored both Duke's and his son Mercer's autobiographies, was there and said that no "jazz artist or group ever had such an impact on an English audience, before or since, as Ellington's band did on that occasion." Not only was the sound incredible, but they did it with a visual style that flabbergasted the audience. In front of the impeccably clad musicians, Bessie "Snake-hips" Dudley performed a highly invigorating and sensual dance number that both inspired the musicians as well as the spectators. Not even Louis Armstrong's performance some months previously, which Dance had witnessed first hand, measured up to Duke's. For one, Armstrong didn't have as strong a band, and the difference between his records and the live performance was enormous, although his trumpet

Duke Ellington and Joya Sherrill. Sherrill sang with the band during World War II, when the Big Band era was peaking. She was considered an excellent vocalist but retired very young.

solos were enthusiastically received.

The Ellington shows were sold out wherever they went. The Prince of Wales even followed the group over to Liverpool, where he bought cheap tickets and sat in the back rather than pull rank to get front row seats—the gesture was appreciated by the working-class audience who cheered the prince along with Duke Ellington.

One fourteen-year-old Turkish boy, the son of the ambassador, couldn't get enough. He later said, "I'd heard Armstrong and Henderson. I'd heard Lew Stone. But I'd never heard anything like this. It changed my life." Later, with his brother, he founded Atlantic Records, one of the most successful jazz and pop labels of all time.

Duke struck up another life-long friendship during the tour. Gene Gertler, the thirteen-year old daughter of the painter, Mark Gertler, somehow got through to Duke on the telephone and said that her father couldn't get tickets for his show, and asked if Duke could help. He did, but said she'd have to phone everyday after she got out of school to wake him up so he wouldn't be late for the show. She did, and the friendship blossomed. She later married Leslie Diamond, and whenever Duke was in London, he stayed with the Diamonds.

After England, they spent time in Holland and Paris, where the reception was even better. The English tour had been marred once when only Duke could get a room at a prestigious hotel because the management didn't want coloreds, and the rest of the band had to be transported to a lower-rent district of London. While the event wasn't anything like the treatment in the states, it proved that racism still existed throughout the world.

In France, Duke's music was hailed as surrealist. It sprang from the unconscious, not the conscious, one critic wrote.

Not only did the 1933 European tour have a great affect on the audiences, inspiring musicians and the population, it fundamentally shifted Duke's own perspective on what he was doing. Before, he was an entertainer. He made people feel good. But the reception and depth of knowledge and critical acclaim speckled with criticism (usually by more earnest minded writers who thought Ellington wasn't taking his music seriously enough!) proved that something else was happening. "That kind of thing gives you courage to go on," Duke later wrote. "If they think I'm that important, then maybe I have said something. Maybe our music does mean something."

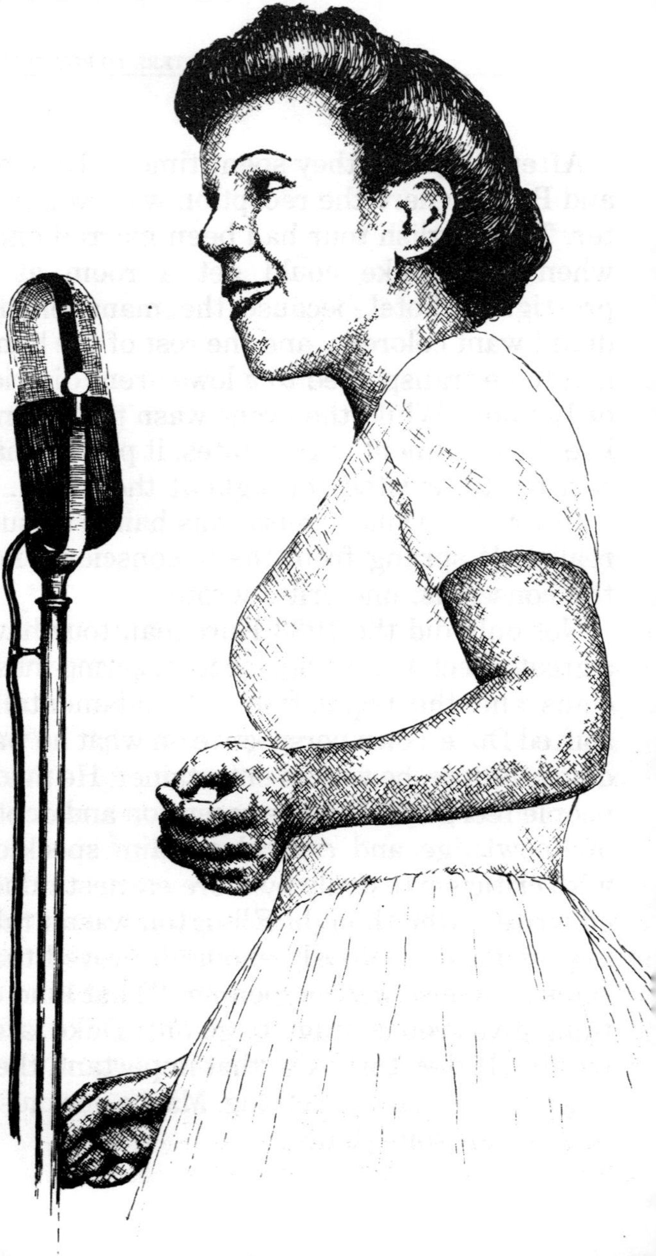

Chapter Five

Roaditis

WHEN THEY RETURNED TO the States, it was back to the old grind of the road tours, but with one big difference. Their popularity had grown to such a degree that Duke was able to pick his engagements more carefully, thus avoiding parts of the country where they'd been badly treated.

After a run at the Chicago Theater during the 1933 World's Fair, however, Duke was hesitant about a tour Mills wanted to book in Texas. It was such good money that Duke, with some reservations, went for it. They, of course, traveled in the two Pullman cars which were

---

Ivie Anderson could be called the first of the Big Band singers. The bands were more important than the singers in that era, and the singer's voice was used much as an instrument.

pulled into side tracks and hooked up to water, electricity and sanitation. On the side, DUKE ELLINGTON was emblazoned, further publicizing the band, and creating something of a sensation wherever he went. They were the only musicians, white or black, who traveled in such a fashion.

Duke was surprised at the reception he got in Texas. "...in a few days I was together with the people and down, as we say, and sounding like a Texan," Duke later wrote. "They had obviously been waiting for us. We made a lot of friends down there, and the climate and environment were conducive to our music."

Duke was invited back three years later to play for the Texas Centennial, which was celebrating all aspects of Texas history: white, Hispanic, Native American, and black. He was honored with a Certificate of Accomplishment, which was not given on basis of race, but on merit only. "We're Western, not Southern," Texans would tell him, at least during a performance. Yet, even Texas in the 30s had segregated hotels, restaurants, and bathrooms. Not as intense as the South, racism still prevailed outside the dance halls.

After the success of the Texas tour, Duke started to accept bookings throughout the Deep South: Louisiana, Alabama, Georgia, and the Carolinas, while still criss-crossing the continent from California to New England.

Life on the road was not easy. Often they were away from their families for six months at a time. The grind of playing one hall, packing and moving to another town just in time to set up and play for another concert, after which they'd have to hurriedly pack up and move again was, at best, tedious. "I have seen men on the bandstand so miserable it hurt me," Duke said about life on the road.

In addition to the physical and emotional strain, the road was incredibly boring. Spending hours cooped up in a rail road car or a bus or in a dingy hotel room in a strange town got too much to handle. The money was excellent, more than they could get doing other jobs. It helped, for a while, but it often wasn't enough to keep all of them traveling.

If a band member asked for a few weeks off and couldn't get it, he'd just quit. Juan Tizol, a regular trombonist with Duke's band for more than 15 years, suddenly blew up during a tour out to the West, and just quit. "I could only be home once a year. So I had to leave. It was the road. It was too long, and I couldn't take it anymore."

Another musician, Taft Jordan, said he slept for an entire year after leaving the band. "I often slept two or three times a day, and not just catnaps, but for two or three hours. I hadn't realized how tired I was while I was out there."

With the strain of travel, the tedium and the boredom causing constant stress on the band, it is little wonder that they took to a variety of diversions to help pass the time. Practical jokes were a staple with the band, and the various musicians were constantly playing tricks on each other. Once some players filled the tuba, which was only occasionally played during the night, with water. Barney Bigard sat in front of it, so when the bassist put down his normal instrument and picked up the tubs, Bigard was drenched in a shower of water in the middle of a performance. The bow of a violinist whose ego was getting out of hand had soap rubbed on it so it wouldn't make a sound when played. Band uniforms got filled with itching powder, creating a nightmare for the victim who couldn't get offstage to sooth himself. Even occasional stink bombs exploded during the middle of a solo performance to unnerve the player. Juan Tizol, an ace practical joker himself, claimed that his taste for such infantile nonsense ended when someone placed a firecracker under his chair during a party at Irving Mills' office.

Mary Lou Williams, one of the few capable female jazz musicians, (other than the singers, of course) arranged compositions for Ellington's band for several years, but got little credit.

Hardwick, when he first joined the band, was the victim of quite an elaborate joke. He was told that the new members had to buy the refreshments for the band's party. He was sent out to purchase some items, then given the address where the party was supposedly to take place—the house of a woman. When he got there, he walked in and found the woman and her angry husband, right behind her. "So that's the guy who's been cheating with my wife!" he screamed, then aimed a gun and fired.

Hardwick dropped the groceries and ran for his life down the sidewalk, right into the back of laughing musicians. It had all been a set up. The gun had been loaded with blanks, and the police were told of the practical joke.

Hardwick, in turn, played one on Freddy Jenkins, who had the habit of licking his mouthpiece before playing his trumpet. Just before a performance one night, Hardwick smeared the trumpeter's favorite mouthpiece with hot peppers.

Even though practical jokes were played during a performance, Duke rarely reprimanded his musicians. He knew that the lifestyle was hard on them, and that a few light moments could break the tension, and help them relax.

They killed time with card games: black jack,

bridge, red dog, pinochle, gin rummy, but the most popular game was stud poker. Surprisingly, one of the consistently best players was Ivie Anderson, the band's singer and only female. She and Duke were noted for their ability to "clean up the table" just about anytime they played.

Alcohol, however, was another problem. While it was the most popular escape from reality, it often created more problems than it solved, usually making life a living hell for everyone else.

It was also, indirectly, what paid their bills. The whole point of someone going to a nightclub was to drink, especially during Prohibition. The entertainment went along with it. The classier clubs had better music but not necessarily better booze.

The rivalry between musicians was sometimes intense, and taken out in a "friendly" drinking contest. Even Duke Ellington was known to be a pretty sturdy drinker, but probably did so to get on the good side of his men, to be "one of the boys." He once joined in on a drinking contest between two trumpeters, Freddy Jenkins and Rex Stewart, who was with another band at the time. When Jenkins and Stewart were too drunk to find their way back to their hotel rooms, Duke showed them the way although he'd downed just as many shots of gin as either of them. In 1940, Duke gave up drinking completely.

For others, the outcome was not so romantic. Even the highly talented Bubber Miley, who died in 1932, had problems with liquor. As Duke tells it, "Bubber used to crawl under the piano and go to sleep whenever he felt like it. In fact, all the horn-blowers were lushes, and I used to have to go around and get them out of bed to get them to work on time."

The saxophonist, Willie Smith, said that alcohol might pick him up when he was bored or sleepy, but after a while, he'd need more and more to keep going. "After a while, it destroys your coordination, your thinking, and everything else. You finally end up a drunkard."

Saxophonist Paul Gonsalves, who joined Ellington in the 50s, was once reputed to have fallen over during the middle of a solo. Later in his life, there was always a constant need to have a stand by soloist ready in case he didn't show up, which happened on a few occasions. One of the few times Duke lost his good-natured temperament in public was over a dispute with Gonsalves, who showed up too drunk to play.

Even with the severe cases, Ellington never actually fired his players. As one musician,

Russell Proscope, put it, "Duke ruled his men with an iron hand in a mink glove." If he had grown to dislike a player, he would stop associating with him. Sometimes, if another continued to show up drunk to a gig too many times, Duke, while praising him, would call on the man to play a number of solos at a frenzied pace, knowing that he would be too drunk to keep up. After a while, the shamed man would get the idea and either quit in humiliation or try to get back on track. He didn't play favorite with his top stars either. Paul Gonsalves and John Hodges (as renowned at the time on the sax as Louis Armstrong was on the trumpet) were both occasionally called on to play encores of solos when they were so hung over they could hardly see straight.

Despite the hardships, life with Duke on the road was, in many ways, better than most of the alternatives. The country, since the crash of 1929, had been plunged into the Great Depression, and one of the few solid paying jobs was for musicians. The tours were Duke's bread-and-butter jobs. Of course, they were mixed in between occasional movie work and short runs at night clubs. He played from time to time at the Hollywood and the Cotton Club, and other theaters.

Duke was as loyal to his musicians as they

were to him. He had a knack for writing a piece of music that was just right for a particular player, and would announce special numbers written especially for one player or another, Cootie's Concerto or Barney's Concerto. He wrote "Trumpet in Spades" for Rex Stewart and "Yearning for Love" for Lawrence Brown.

Harry Carney, for example, played the Baritone sax, but he had such a rich tone that he could play notes in the range of a tenor, and Duke would give him some of the high parts. If another baritone saxophonist tried it, it wouldn't sound right because he wouldn't be Harry Carney.

With such narrowly tailored music, it was no wonder many of the musicians at first thought that Ellington's music was weird, but once it was played, it had a strangely compelling affect, especially on the audiences. Loyalty to Duke was quite intense, several members staying with him as long as twenty years, and a few for as long as forty. Johnny Hodges and Harry Carney stayed with Ellington from the late 20s to the 70s, except for a few years where both created bands of their own with some success.

The road was something working musicians had to put up with if they were dedicated to decent music. "The road is a way of life and you conform to it," Russell Proscope, a saxophonist/clarinetist, once said. "After a while you get to like it."

While the bandmen, for the most part, grew increasingly tired during a tour, the opposite seemed to happen with Duke. He loved traveling, often finding inspiration while on the road. He'd see a grouping of lush hills that would remind him of a reclining woman, and that would be enough to create a melody. The flight of a flock of geese would stimulate another piece of music. A catchy advertising phrase on a billboard would lead him to experiment with similar sounding words, and soon he'd have a tune for another song. Everything inspired him: the sounds of the trains leaving and entering a station, the constant humming of the steel wheels on the iron tracks, the engine whistle of the train, or the glowing fires of an industrial park in Ohio. Duke often thought of music in terms of color, which was undoubtedly due to his talents as a painter. "I like to see flames licking yellow in the dark then pushing down to a red glow," Duke said. Songs named for colors are testament to this: "Mood Indigo," "Azure," "Turquoise Cloud," "Tan and Beige Fantasy," "Black Butterfly," and "Sepia Panorama," to name a few.

Even childhood memories would come to him. "Sophisticated Lady" was about three of Duke's school teachers. After the winter and spring sessions, they would take a trip to Europe for the summer, and that, Duke thought, was very sophisticated.

The Pullman, either rolling or parked, was a place where his thoughts could come into focus. He had the uncanny ability to block out the other bandmen, as if they weren't there, even though they might be playing a boisterous game of poker.

His sister, Ruth, once said, "You'd see him in a siding in Texas. The heat might be at 110 and sweat pouring off him onto a piece of manuscript paper on his knee, but he'd act as if it were a cool 70, trying to finish a tune."

Duke was famous for his habit of pulling out a scrap of paper and jotting notes and ideas down, often working for hours, or, sometimes for only fifteen minutes. Once Rex Stewart, the noted trumpeter, observed Ellington suddenly tear to pieces and flush down a toilet a composition he'd been working on for hours. When he asked him why he did that, Duke said, "Well, I'll tell you, Fat Stuff. If it's good, I'll remember it. If it's bad, well I want to forget it and I would prefer that no one catches on to how lousy I can write."

Duke Ellington leaving the privacy of his Pullman car. For the major portion of his career, his bands traveled by private Pullman which saved the hassle of where to sit and sleep.

One reason for his stamina was his obsession with health. He was something of a hypochondriac, undoubtedly a carry over from his overly concerned mother. He carried a battery of vitamins, pills and an assortment of medication for every possibility. Whenever he felt the least bit down, he would call up a doctor, and later, his private physician, Arthur Logan, from anywhere he happened to be, even from across the globe. He met Dr. Logan during a run at the Cotton Club in 1937, when one of the band members fell sick. Duke and Logan hit it off very well, and became life-long friends. Aside from being a renowned physician, Logan, a very light skinned African-American, was also a civil rights campaigner, and took an active part in political issues.

Although it was a battle, Duke was able to get by financially during the 30s. What helped were his hit tunes. In 1933 he wrote the hit "Sophisticated Lady," and the recording was a big seller. Other hits from the 30s included "Mood Indigo," Drop Me Off in Harlem," "It Don't Mean a Thing If It Ain't Got That Swing," "Solitude," "In a sentimental Mood," and the very exotic "Caravan."

In 1932 Duke's mother contracted cancer. After some consultation, they decided that it was best to send her to Detroit for treatment, but she grew steadily worse. Duke cut down his engagements so he could be with her, but by 1935 it was looking very grim. For three days solid, he stood by her, as did the other members of his family, until she passed away.

It was a catastrophic blow. Duke's whole life had revolved around his mother. In 1930, during his Cotton Club run, he had moved his entire family up to New York so they could be close. It plunged him into a depression that lasted, according to Mercer Ellington, for almost a year. "He just sat around the house and wept for days at a time," Mercer wrote. "This great loss affected his musical output more than anything else that happened in his career. He lost his ambition because he had lost the person he most liked to please."

For the first time in years, he started having financial problems. After his mother died, with fewer tours and no new numbers, Duke had to borrow money against future songs just to keep his band together.

It was still some months before he recovered, but out of his grief emerged an unusual new number, "Reminiscing in Tempo." It was, in some ways, a tonic poem in memory of his mother. It was also very long. It took up both sides of two 78 rpm records, each released through a different company.

Although it was not greatly received at the time, it used even more innovative harmonies and tones than "Creole Rhapsody." The critics were currently on a rave about Benny Goodman music, and "Reminiscing" was anything but a dance tune. One British reviewer called it a "monstrosity," and it was generally poorly received by the critics. "That was unimportant to me," Duke countered in his autobiography, "because I had written my statement. Hearing it constituted my total reward, and in it was a detailed account of my aloneness after losing my mother."

Two years later, his father, who had been managing the band for a while, also passed away. It was another emotional blow.

Through the hardships of the 30s, Duke not only kept the band together, but it was a very creative period, both for the music he created and the musicians he developed. Duke had a good ear for talent. He was reluctant to hire stars away from other bands, but rather preferred to develop his own. Bubber Miley (trumpet), Johnny Hodges (sax), Barney Bigard (clarinet and sax), Harry Carney (baritone sax), Juan Tizol (trombone), Rex Stewart (trumpet) and Cootie Williams (trumpet) all reached the pinnacle, at one time or another, of the jazz world, becoming outright stars. They also contributed greatly to Duke's compositions. They'd make up a riff or a fragment of a melody, and Duke would hear it and suddenly they'd have a collaboration. Duke was also generous, although sometimes inaccurate according to Rex Stewart, in giving his musicians credit for the music.

In the decades that followed, however, such creative collaborations with band members diminished, as he wrote more exclusively with co-composers, and began writing larger arrangements, pushing the sound of his band closer to the symphonic category, but never quite leaving the world of jazz.

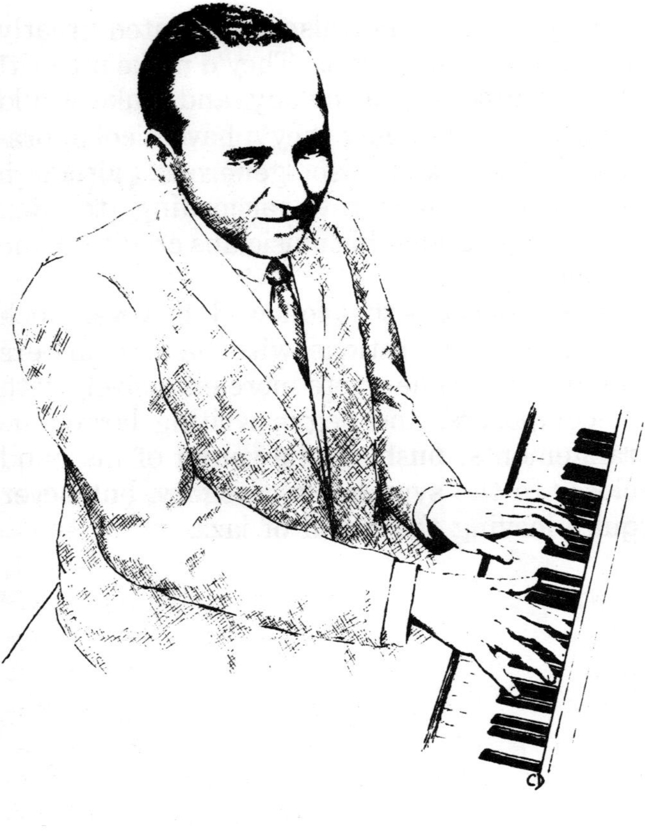

―――― *Chapter Six* ――――

The Rollercoaster of Success

B Y THE MID 30s, a new music craze, a style of jazz called swing, was suddenly sweeping the nation.

While Duke was developing his "jungle" music at the cotton club, another band run by Fletcher Henderson, which included renowned trumpeter Louis Armstrong among others, started playing jazz with a stronger dance rhythm that had more of a swing to it. Unfortunately the band soon broke apart, but not before Benny Goodman absorbed the flavor of the music. In 1935, he played several new arrangements in Los Angeles, and the music was

Early bandleader Fletcher Henderson employed many great musicans, such as Louis Armstrong. He, too, played a rather cool jazz and Duke Ellington became his competition.

a hit. Within months, teenagers all over the country were hooked, and big bands were even more popular than ever.

Although Ellington's band had been playing similar music—he wrote "It Don't Mean a Thing If it Ain't Got That Swing" in 1932—it was richer and more subtle than Goodman's dance numbers. Duke also loved other styles. He played ballads and very experimental music, so his music was not always easy to dance to. In fact, some young fans, not acquainted with the musical traditions of the time, didn't even consider Duke Ellington swing music at all.

Soon, however, with the popularity and record sales of swing music skyrocketing, Ellington's studio dates started picking up.

The new Big Band sound was so popular, with such high profile styles of playing, some promoter somewhere came up with the idea of pitting two bands against each other during the same dance to see which one was the best, judged, of course, by the dancers themselves. It was the "Battle of the Bands" craze.

To "cut" another band was to out play them either with variety of solos, the speed of the music, or how fast they moved from one tune to the next. It was like a shark feeding frenzy; instead of fish, the dancers and musicians devoured the music.

Duke Ellington wasn't keen on battle-of-the-bands contests, and only rarely showed up to participate. But when he did, he made sure he was up for the competition. At the time, Chick Webb's wild group were considered the best swing band in Harlem. Duke was invited to the Savoy Ballroom for a battle. After Webb opened to a enthusiastic audience, he felt Duke didn't have a chance, but once he started playing, and churned out number after number, working the crowd into a dancing fury. Chick, according to one of his own bandmen, sneaked out of the ballroom, too embarrassed to hear anymore. "This was the first time we'd been really washed out. They outswung us, they out-everythinged us," Webb's trombonist, Sandy Williams, said of the event.

As Duke played more swing numbers, he didn't turn his back on other forms of music. Rather, he always offered a wide range of styles and moods in his performances.

While he'd never been schooled in music, he was interested in symphonic sounds. By chance, he happened to meet a young stock broker named Edmund Anderson who was trying to break into the music business. He and Ellington became good friends. Music critics at the time were comparing Ellington to the likes of Delius, Ravel and Debussy, but he'd never really had a chance to listen to them. Once in fact, Duke had been invited to a lecture at a New York university. The professor had claimed that Ellington was heavily influenced by Delius. Rather than show up and embarrass the professor, Duke went to a music shop and bought everything he could find on the guy so he could at least say he'd listened to his music.

Anderson and Duke spent many afternoons together listening to Anderson's symphonic records. Duke would hear a section and exclaim, "Say, that's a rumba!" Or he'd hear an incredibly imaginative oboe solo and say, "Man listen to him climb!" He was impressed with the way symphonic music was both colorful and picturesque, and began to absorb it into his own music. In 1936 he shared the billing with members of the New York Philharmonic who played music by modern French and Russian avant-garde composers for society people at the St. Regis Hotel.

The band was also appearing in Hollywood movies, and Ivie Anderson, his regular singer, was featured in the Marx Brother's "A Day at the Races," for which Duke also wrote some of the music.

Beatrice Ellis ("Evie Ellington") became Duke's companion in 1938 and they lived together in a New York apartment until his death in 1974. She died soon afterwards.

Things were about as good as they could get in the States, but a date at the Carnegie Hall still eluded him. Benny Goodman, however, had made it there within a couple of years after igniting the swing craze.

Duke had been wanting to go back to Europe where he felt he was "really" appreciated.

In Europe, race had little to do with how well his music was received. Duke attempted to explain the almost mystic attraction Europe had to an African-American musician. "Europe is a different world. You can go anywhere, do anything, talk to anybody. You are like a guy who has eaten hot dogs all his life and is suddenly offered caviar. You can't believe it."

In a magazine article written in the 60s, Rex Stewart recalled an incident in Sweden where 5,000 school children came out to serenade Duke's birthday. An even great irony, however, was that even African-Americans didn't regard Duke's music as highly as did the Europeans. "The American Negro by and large couldn't care less about Ellington's music, and considers it old hat and not in his groove," Stewart also wrote. No matter what he did, experimental or religious or dance music, it was always labeled "jazz" in the commercial world.

Even more ironic, in most music stores today, one has to go to the "Big Band" section, where Duke has been further regulated to "swing" music.

In 1939, despite the political turmoil, Duke finally got a chance to return. Due to a British Musicians' Union ban on American jazz players, they were unable to get a single booking in England. They started in Paris with much acclaim, then on to Holland and Denmark.

While Europe greeted Duke with passion, Germany was another case. Duke had heard that its leader, Adolf Hitler, had banned all jazz because it was music from a lesser race.

It was with great anxiety that Duke discovered that they would have to travel through Germany in order to get to Denmark. In Hamburg, they had a six hour layover—a painful six hours as 20 some odd black people waited around for the next train, fearing from second to second that the worst would suddenly happen. They were "strangely ignored," Duke wrote years later. On the train, however, a group of youngsters who saw the record player and asked if they had some jazz records they could hear. "They played those records all day," Duke wrote, "with the volume turned up loud enough to wake people in other parts of the train."

In Copenhagen, Denmark, Duke found yet other German youths who'd sneaked out of their country so they could listen to the "banned" music.

The reception in Sweden was exceptional. The Grand Hotel gave a huge birthday party for Duke that began at 8 a.m., and every employee, from the head manager to the dishwasher, lined up to greet him. The festivities continued all day, and during two evening concerts given in his honor, capped with 5,000 youths first singing a birthday song in Swedish, then a chorus of young girls rendering it in English. It was as close to paradise as Duke ever got. There was, unfortunately, one dark spot. Hitler was making daily radio broadcasts, threatening the Swedes and the rest of Europe. It was so chilling, Duke and Rex Stewart both wanted to take the next boat home.

The tour was eventually cut short due to the Nazi aggression, and Duke and his orchestra were soon back in New York, keeping a safe distance as world war ignited across the Atlantic.

As the world was preparing for war, Duke's band underwent a few more changes that, incredibly enough, improved it another notch. Some jazz critics say that the Ellington band of the early 40s was the best of all. For sheer performance abilities of its soloists, there's much merit to the statement. The addition of new members—Billy Strayhorn, Ben Webster, and Jimmy Blanton in 1939—had the biggest impact on the band since its Cotton Club days.

The greatest influence on Duke was Billy Strayhorn, who wasn't an instrumentalist at all, although he did play the piano quite well. That wasn't his talent; writing was.

Duke had met Billy Strayhorn through a friend, who said that he wrote "good music." Not thinking much of it because he'd heard that line thousands of times over the years, Duke listened half-heartedly to the young man between performances while in Pittsburgh. But mid-way through his first song, Duke was all ears. He was stunned at the perfect blend of music and words that this young man had come up with. Duke listened to the songs several times, taking up the entire break between programs. He wanted to hear more, and have the boy write lyrics for him, but in the confusion of getting back on stage he forgot to get his address.

Several months later Strayhorn showed up the day before Duke left for the 1939 European tour. Duke introduced him to his son, Mercer, and sister, Ruth—who, being only a

Duke Ellington with members of his band backstage at the Hurricane Club, May, 1943. Congenial enough on the surface, Ellington kept a distance between himself and his players, even Sonny

Greer, who was with him from the beginning, was always referred to by his full name in conversation. Oddly, Ellington treated his son, Mercer, in much the same manner.

couple of years older than Mercer was more a sister than an aunt to the young man. He told Mercer to take care of the young man while they were away.

Mercer arranged for a room at the YMCA. He had just organized a small band and was trying to write some original music, and Strayhorn offered to help. They worked on some numbers together, and, wanting to learn all they could about musical compositions, they rummaged through Duke's scores, studying them intensely to try and figure out what he was doing. Strayhorn had a fairly solid grounding in music. In fact, he had never intended getting into jazz music in the first place. He was a classicist. He played in his school's orchestra and studied the great composers, Bach, Beethoven and Brahms. As a musician, he didn't think he was good enough to make a decent living at it, but he loved music, and studied it passionately. Like Duke, he was very fortunate in finally being able to make a living at his hobby.

Before he encountered Duke, Billy Strayhorn would have been content with music as just a hobby, studying the classics for the rest of his life, but one evening he happened to stumble onto Duke's concert in Pittsburgh. It completely changed his outlook on jazz.

During the program, Duke had played his free adaptation of Franz List's "Hungarian Rhapsody," which he called "Ebony Rhapsody." He'd written it 1934 it for the film "Murder at the Vanities," but it was so popular he often included it in his performances. It really shook the young Billy Strayhorn up. "I was lost," he later said about that first encounter with Ellington's music.

By the time Duke returned, Strayhorn had moved in with Mercer and Ruth, and had joined Mercer's band. The three were already so much like a family that Duke just naturally became a father to them all.

When Strayhorn commented that he thought he could do some orchestrating, Duke took it in stride, but it wasn't until he was short a few numbers for a recording date, that he asked Strayhorn to orchestrate some tunes, knowing that he would be able to "fix" them during the session if he had to. As soon as the band played Strayhorn's arrangements, they were stunned. They couldn't understand how someone so young could write something that elegant and moving. They dubbed him "Sweetpea," after the kid in the "Popeye" comics because Strayhorn was so tiny and so lovable, and everyone instantly liked him.

Duke quickly pulled Strayhorn into the band,

and the two began a collaboration that lasted right up to Strayhorn's death in 1967. Part of the reason for the success of their collaboration was that they were both on the same wave length musically. Years later, when Duke was composing his first Sacred Concert, he asked Billy to come up with something for an introduction. They were each on opposite sides of the continent, but when they finally met, their themes were almost identical. "Any time I was in the throes of debate with myself, harmonically or melodically, I would turn to Strays. We would talk, and then the whole world would come into focus."

While Duke often listened and used what his musicians come up with during impromptu sessions, and sometimes collaborated with them on a song here and there, Strayhorn was something much more. Not only did they have a long list of compositions together, including several of the longer works and other adaptations of classics, but Duke began to rely heavier on Strayhorn than he had any other person except his mother. It was like a love affair, a love affair of music, and Duke was motivated to try to please the young man. Strayhorn, in turn, tried to impress Duke with his knowledge of music and good judgment.

Otto Hardwick commented later about Duke

and Strayhorn, "Neither money nor business was an issue between them ever. Billy just wanted to be with Duke, and that was all."

Their working relationship, like jazz, was not structured. Sometimes Strayhorn would travel with the band, even relieve Duke at the piano during a performance. Sometimes he'd stay home working on arrangements Duke asked him to do, or he'd just work on some ideas he'd been thinking about on his own. His "Take the 'A' Train," quickly became the band's new theme song and, with the ballad "Lust Life," Strayhorn's compositions were becoming hits.

Although both were very close musically, there was still a difference. Duke's music was still more improvisational, primitive in the good sense of jazz music. It had raw-edged emotion. Strayhorn, on the other hand, was more structured, more polished and smoother. He was also the main force behind the adaptations of classic symphonies that would later be highly acclaimed throughout the 60s. Their strength was in discussing what they thought was the best approach to a piece. "The actual writing was nothing," Strayhorn said in an interview with Stanley Dance. It was the preparation that took the time. When they were adapting "The Nutcracker Suite," by Tchaikovsky, they talked it over for six months

It took Duke Ellington years to be invited to play at Carnegie Hall, but it finally happened on January 23, 1943. No black group had been invited before Ellington. And since Carnegie was

then the most prestigious concert hall in America, Ellington realized playing there was a tremendously opportunity to have his music taken seriously.

trying to decide which instruments should play which parts and how they should play it. Once they figured it out, the writing took only a few days.

Ben Webster, the other addition in 1939, was important because it marked the first time Duke featured the tenor sax as a solo instrument. He hadn't done it before, because he hadn't run across a remarkable tenor saxophonist. Webster had done a few guest appearances with the band, and sat in on a recording session in 1935, but it wasn't until 1939 that Duke was able to afford him full time. The addition filled out the reed section, giving it more variety and power.

A short while after Strayhorn and Webster joined, they came across a very unusual 19-year-old bass player named Jimmy Blanton. They were playing in St. Louis at the time, and although Duke had already gone to bed, Strayhorn and Webster absolutely insisted that Duke immediately pull on a coat over his pajamas and rush over to a hotel ballroom to listen to this phenomenon. The kid was doing things to the bass fiddle that no one had done before. He was playing it like a solo instrument. Up to that time, the bass string simply played the four basic beats, keeping the rhythm like the drums. About the only thing

Duke had done with the instrument was hire two instead of one, in order to get more sound out of it. Recently, one of the bassists had quit, so Duke was down to one again.

Jimmy Blanton was playing an outright melody line on the bass, plucking frantically with his fingers and the bow to create a stunning new sound. Duke offered him a job that night, and he joined Duke full time.

After a couple of months, the other bassist, in the middle of a dance in Boston, finally had all he could take, packed up his instrument and walked out. "I can't stand next to someone playing that good night after night; it's too embarrassing."

What Blanton did with the bass, soon became a staple with every jazz band at one time or another. It was another case of jazz opening up an instrument, such as the saxophone, to a rich new world of ideas.

Blanton's career, unfortunately, quickly ended in tragedy. Within two years he'd contracted tuberculosis and died in 1942, but not before setting the musical world on end with his innovative bass fiddling.

In 1940, Cootie Williams, one of the all time stars of the Ellington band, quit to join Benny Goodman's band. It came as such a shock to Duke's fans, that another composer actually wrote a song called "When Cootie Left the Duke." In actuality, Duke knew that Cootie wanted to further develop his trumpet playing, and Goodman was one of the top bands in the country. Duke even helped negotiate Cootie's salary, making sure the young man got paid what he deserved. Duke shrugged off the affair saying, as he always did, "He'll be back."

A year later, Williams quit Goodman, but it was to form his own band, not rejoin Duke. Williams either hired or developed or lent a helping hand to such renowned musicians as Charlie Parker, Thelonius Monk (who wrote "Round Midnight"), and the famous Pearl Bailey when they were just getting started.

Eventually, however, Duke turned out to be right. Twenty-two years later, Williams did in fact return, after having climbed to the big time and then crashing into the skids.

Coincidentally, the day after Williams left, Duke happened to run across another exquisite trumpet player at a small club. He was a pintsized young man from Chicago named Ray Nance. Not only did he play the trumpet and cornet, he could handle a violin with flair, and sing and dance. He was soon nicknamed "Floorshow" because of the variety of his talents, all of which he somehow managed to fit into a solo.

Duke and Irving Mills finally went their separate ways in 1940. Duke traded his interest in the Cab Calloway band (which was his relief band during his tenure at the Cotton Club) for Mills' share of the Ellington band. Mills also retained rights to a number of Ellington hits.

Even after the breakup, Mills continued to receive co-credit for songs written as late as 1962.

Duke signed up with the William Morris Agency, which did the same sort of one-night bookings for his cross-country tours.

By 1940, Duke Ellington had assembled the best musicians yet, and, with the aid of Billy Strayhorn, was writing the most vigorous and technically proficient music of his life. The hits were streaming out: "Jack The Bear," "Bojangles," "Ko Ko," "In a Mellotone," "Warm Valley," "Sepia Panorama," "Don't Get Around Much Anymore," and "Harlem Airshaft" were a few of the more notable ones. Also remarkable was the variety of the songs. Some were portraits. "Bojangles" was in honor of the famous dancer, Bill Robinson. "Harlem Airshaft" attempted to capture the flavor of the sounds of an apartment building in the middle of Harlem. "Jack The Bear" featured the highly original bass fiddler, Jimmy Blanton .

Things just couldn't get much better, so Duke branched out into a new area: Theater. It started Duke on yet a new venture in music: extended works and concert shows. It would be a passion that stayed with him right up to the very end. He was no longer interested in just writing hit tunes; he wanted to say something with his music. Enlarge the audience, give them musical images celebrating the folk traditions of the African-American experience.

The idea for the first musical began during a short stay in Los Angeles in 1941. He'd made friends with several people in Hollywood when he was working on "Cabin in the Sky" (featuring Lena Horne). Orson Welles was one of his most fanatical devotees, and other celebrities who respected him included Mickey Rooney, Lana Turner, Jackie Cooper, and Tony Martin.

Duke met with a group of Hollywood writers, including the renowned poet and novelist, Langston Hughes. They felt they wanted to correct the racial problem in America through a theatrical play. It would be called "Jump for Joy," and it was quite extraordinary and quite a radical example of "message theater" for the time. It was a

Lena Horne and Duke Ellington admired each other professionally, but for whatever reason, they were never all that close personally. "Duke just didn't like women," said son, Mercer.

celebration of Negro music and culture while at the same time trying to destroy the stereotype images of blacks.

The original opening had Uncle Tom dying in a hospital bed, with a chorus of black singers "jumping for joy" now that the Uncle Tom stereotype was dying. Flanked on either side of the sickly old man was a Hollywood movie mogul and a Broadway theater producer injecting adrenalin into his arms to keep him alive.

Many ideas were even more sardonic, and had to be cut out of fear of going too far. Even during the run, as soon as the curtain fell, the writers would gather with Duke and the producers and discuss what worked and didn't work, and what might be too offensive. A number which had three blacks working in a tailor shop singing Jewish songs was cut after the first night even though it had been quite a success.

"Jump for Joy" also featured Duke as an actor, not just a band leader or piano player. Dorothy Dandrige and Herb Jeffries were two of the featured stars of the enormous cast.

During its three month run, it played to standing room only. The audience was made up of members of all the racial groups in Los Angeles, from Hollywood celebrities to professional blacks (lawyers, doctors, bankers), to street hustlers. Duke wrote that all the blacks would come out of the theater with their chests puffed out and beaming proudly.

After three months, the show was upstaged by a much bigger event: World War II. The Japanese had bombed Pearl Harbor, and suddenly America was at war. Many members of the cast were suddenly drafted, leaving too big of a gap to fill, and the show was forced to close.

The feelings it inspired, however, lingered on, and Cress Courtney of the William Morris Agency told Ellington to write a long work, like a concert. "...and let's do it in Carnegie Hall," he added.

At that time, no black jazz or swing band had ever played at Carnegie Hall.

At the time, Duke was in a theater in Hartfort. The warm up act for Ellington was a young singer with a bright future ahead of himself, Frank Sinatra. (Years later, Sinatra would hire Duke to do the musical score for "Assault on a Queen.") Between the music, the theater showed a horror movie, "The Cat Woman," and Duke would sit near the screen and start jotting some ideas down for what would soon be his first concert performance, "Black, Brown and Beige."

It was a celebration of the history of black music, from the slave days right up to the present. Because it was going to be presented as a concert and not a dance, Ellington was free to experiment as much as he wanted. He went so far out for the time, bridging the gap between the classic symphonic tradition and jazz that critics of either group simply had nothing to compare it to. It wasn't jazz because it was too structured, like symphonic music. It didn't always have a strong, regular beat, and many sections didn't have a "swing" to it. On the other hand, it wasn't a symphonic orchestra playing, either. It was a jazz-swing band with strange sounds and melodies. The public, however, loved it. It also established Duke Ellington as more than just a big band leader, more than a pop songwriter. He was an American folk composer, and he had serious music to present to the public. He was clearly in a class by himself. It was also a chance to express the situation of black Americans to large white audiences.

Duke later said, "I have two careers. One as a band leader and another as a composer. Sometimes I compose for my band and other times I compose for other people." "Blue Bells of Harlem" and "Blutopia" were written exclusively for Paul Whiteman, for example.

Years later, as the cultural revolution exploded with the rise of black pride in the 60s, Duke Ellington was often criticized for not taking an active part in political activities. It was criticism largely unjustified. Ellington had always been deeply concerned, and confronted more than his share of bigotry and hatred ever since he started his music career in the 20s. "People who think that haven't been listening to our music," he later wrote about the criticism. "For the past twenty-five years, social protest and pride of the Negro have been the most significant themes in what we've done..."

Duke's approach was more subtle than many wanted at the time. He felt that by celebrating African-American culture through music in a positive manner, thereby instilling a sense of pride in their heritage, it could do more good in the long run than grabbing a rifle and waving it around making a speech. That's not to say he was against the political activities of the 60s; it wasn't his style.

The Carnegie concerts were completely sold out for the entire run. Other than the New York and Boston performances of "Black, Brown and Beige," the concert was never played again as a whole because of the heavy criticism, but much of it was recorded following year.

After his Carnegie Hall performance, despite the mixed reviews, Duke's major focus was on the larger works, and would remain so for the next three decades.

Carnegie Hall invited Ellington back for yearly concerts that lasted until 1950, motivating him into composing at least one major work per year. The more noted ones were "New World A-Comin'" (1943), "The Perfume Suite" (1946), and "The Deep South Suite" (1947). In 1948 he came out with "The Liberian Suite" and in 1955 came "Harlem." The last two were commissioned works. The Liberian government hired Duke to compose a concert for its centennial. The NBC Symphony wanted Duke to write something for them and his band to perform together, and the remarkably colored and eloquent "Harlem" emerged.

The Carnegie performances got Duke the job of writing the music for an adaptation of John Gay's "The Beggar's Opera" called "Beggar's Holiday." It was remarkable in that the casting was done strictly by ability, not The love interest was between a white a black girl, both playing British

music director, however, didn't

When he made this Voice of American broadcast in 1945 Duke was already known all over the world by his records. He spent the last two decades of his life traveling, giving concerts.

get along very well. He was constantly asked to write more songs, and finally ended up doing almost 80, but only 39 were used. The show turned out to be quite long, three-and-a-half hours, causing another rift between Ellington and the musical director. Duke wanted an hour and a half cut, but he didn't get his way. The result was that while the critics were impressed with the scope of the production, and its biracial casting, it didn't play well with the public. It was just too long.

Despite the prestige of his concerts, in 1943 Duke began to encounter yet more problems. The war was taking its toll. Travel was torturous in peace time, but with the undependable train schedules, gas rationing, and lack of world tours, Ellington's band was forced to not only play the same clubs over and over, but to go to less lucrative dance halls.

The recording sessions were a strong source of revenue, and they put out an impressive number of albums from 1940 to 1942. A dispute between the record companies and the American Federation of Musicians put a hold an all commercial recordings from the fall of 1942 to the end of 1944, causing Duke Ellington to take an enormous financial beating.

Exhausted with the hardships, the talented reed player, Barney Bigard, left the band, and was replaced with Jimmy Hamilton. Because Duke wrote songs so specifically designed for certain players, when they left, their featured songs were also retired. Sometimes they were adapted later on to fit a new player, but generally there would be a break in period before a player could take up the slack left by a featured soloist, and it took a while before Jimmy Hamilton fully took Bigard's place.

With the declining income, and juggling of players, Duke was hit hard. While the concerts didn't give him huge revenues, they increased his prestige and he was able to get booked into the good halls and land radio shows, but even then, times were tough.

Near the end of 1943, while playing at the highly esteemed Hurricane Club, Ellington went into the William Morris office to see if he could borrow $500 to get by on until he got payed by the Hurricane Club. As he went inside, a clerk said that he'd had just received a letter for him. He opened it up and thought he read $2,250 as the amount, and he was jubilant. He wouldn't need to borrow the $500 after all, but then he realized that maybe he read the number wrong. Instead of $2,250, maybe it was only $250. So he looked at it again, and noticed that, indeed, he'd read the wrong amount, but in the other direction. It was for $22,500! It was a royalty check from a popular band that'd recorded one of his songs. The band was the Ink Spots.

Ellington hoped that once the recording ban was lifted, he could get back on his feet. When it ended, Duke found himself with yet another problem: Bebop.

The record companies were scrambling to hire musicians who played this new rage in jazz: Charlie Parker, Dizzy Gillespie (who played with Ellington for a few months), Thelonious Monk, Kenny Clarke, Bud Powell. The groups were smaller than big bands, more intimate, playing a more improvisational style and less orchestrated jazz. It was, in some ways, a trend back to early jazz, less coloring and shading of sound, and more soul and power playing.

Additionally, a revival of Dixieland jazz, the white brand of King Oliver's New Orleans brass jazz band, was hot. Ellington found himself in the middle ground. Too big to be bebop and too recent to be Dixieland.

For the first time in over a decade, Duke Ellington found himself outside the cutting edge of music.

Unlike other trends, Duke had no interest in adapting his band to fit the popular forms. He'd witnessed how swing had turned many into mediocre bands, churning out uninspired songs just to make money. Publishers used to come to Ellington with uninteresting songs and say, "Let us put your name on this and you'll make a lot of money." But Duke didn't want to be associated with a mediocre tune, knowing that in the long run, it would ruin whatever reputation he'd built up over the years.

Rather than flow with the times, Duke went against the grain. He persisted with his band, but continued to work on the concert pieces, the extended works.

By 1947, the big bands of Benny Goodman, Tommy Dorsey, Benny Carter, and Woody Herman had all folded. Count Basie was hit hard, and he'd eventually go under, but resurface later.

Yet, Ellington held on with a kind of neurotic madness. "It's a matter of whether you want to play music or make money," he said. "I like to keep a band so I can write and hear the music the next day."

Another dispute halted recording dates in 1948, further depressing the band. Unlike the start of the decade where everything seemed to go Duke's way, at the end of the 40s everything seemed to go wrong. Hardwick and Ben Webster both left in 1946, each claiming that they'd had enough of life on the road. Trombonist Tricky Sam Nanton, one of the original virtuosos of the mute, fell sick and passed away.

Then Duke became ill, and had to undergo surgery to remove a cyst from one of his kidneys. He went to England to recuperate, and took trumpeter Ray "Floorshow" Nance and singer Kay Davis with him.

Even during this informal tour, Duke still had an entourage of personalities with him. He also had his barber and a recent millionaire, Jack Robbins, who'd just sold his music publishing company and was retained as a president with no responsibilities for a $100,000 a year. He had nothing to do so Duke invited him along for the ride. About the only thing he did that could even remotely be called work was carry the barber's bag.

In England, after gathering his strength again following the surgery, he made a few appearances with Nance and Davis. Rather than being a time of rest and peace for him, Duke was confronted with two sets of problems.

As he tried out numbers from his more serious concerts, they didn't go over well in Europe. His fans revolted. They wanted the "traditional" Ellington jazz, the "Black and Tan Fantasy," "Caravan." The hits from before the war. While they were more educated in jazz than the U.S. public, they were also more demanding and, as the 50s approached, more stagnant and resistant to new forms of music. While this would eventually change, there was a strong nostalgia running through Europe in the late 40's. The music of Duke Ellington brought back memories of better times, and they demanded the old hits.

News that some members of his band were tearing up in Harlem started trickling in. Billy Strayhorn, Jimmy Hamilton, Sonny Greer, and more recent additions to the band, Russell Procope and Al Hibbler were playing at the Apollo Bar on 125th Street, doing their own music and were creating quite a sensation.

When Duke Ellington headed back to New York, he didn't even know if he was still going to have a band to return to.

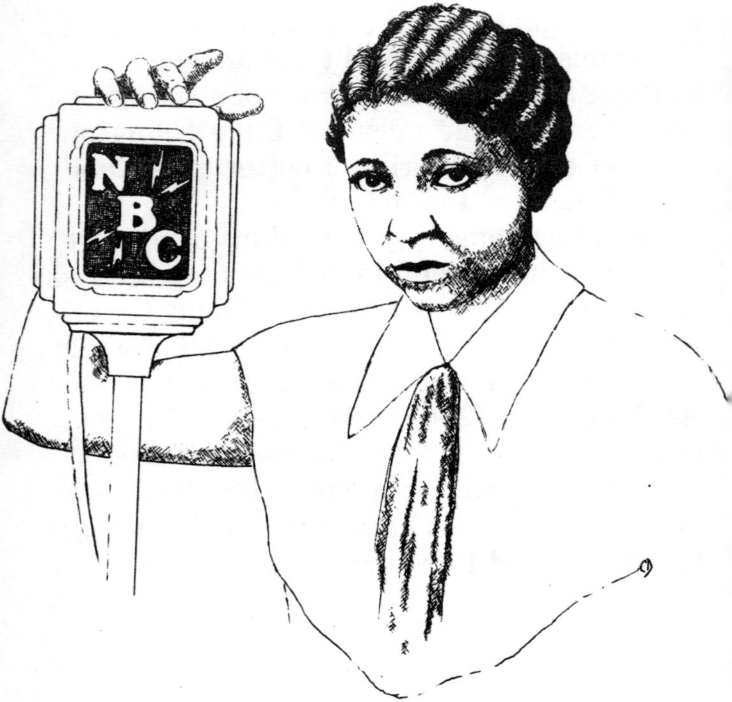
NBC

---------- Chapter Seven ----------

Rebound

WHEN DUKE ARRIVED BACK in New York, he went straight to the Apollo Bar and to find out whether or not his players were breaking away. They'd been so successful, and the routine was so enjoyable, that there was some discussion between them before they made up their minds. Their loyalty to Duke won out and Duke was still in business, but the situation was, at best, grim.

With swing out and bebop or old style Dixieland jazz in, Duke seemed to have lost his audience. At least the youth. Even record companies were hesitant about doing new Duke

Though their careers went in wildly different directions in later years, with Ethel Waters turning almost entirely to acting, in the early days she was Duke's favorite singer.

Ellington numbers because they were afraid they'd bomb. The only recording deals he could land were for his old favorites.

The road was getting harder and harder to find decent bookings. Duke dipped into his royalty money to keep the band on payroll, but by 1951, with morale low, they weren't as sharp as they had been before. They were missing cues, often sluggish and lackadaisical. The band wasn't in sync, and it seemed just a matter of time before things would completely fall apart.

He even tried another European tour in 1950 through Scandinavia and France. When his dearest friends, the Diamonds, met him in Paris, they reprimanded Duke for how shabby he'd let the band become. In 1933, it sparkled with neat suits and impressive music; now, they had wrinkled suits, mismatched instruments—silver ones mixed in with brass-gold.

He was warmly received in Europe, and played very well. They may have looked shabby, but they were happy to be with a grateful audience, and gave them their all, despite the mumbling and grumblings that went on behind the scenes. On stage, they played their hearts out. The audiences were quite pleased with the Ellington orchestra, but to Duke it was still a disappointing success because most of what they played was his old music. That's what the audience came to hear and demanded even though Ellington would try numbers from his newer, more mature music, like "The Liberian Suite."

A rift had also opened up between Duke and his long-time friend, Sonny Greer. Sonny'd become more and more unreliable because of his drinking problem. In Paris, they had a shouting argument over money, and Greer called him a "son of a bitch." The phrase being much stronger in the 50s than it is today, severely insulted Duke because he took it as a comment on his mother. While Duke rarely held a grudge against a band member, he was never able to forgive Greer for the outburst.

When they arrived back in the states, Duke performed his "Harlem" suite in tandem with the NBC symphonic under the direction of Arturo Tascanni at the Metropolitan Opera House. It was a charity concert for the NAACP. Ellington proved he could write for a symphonic orchestra, but when asked by reporters if he'd do more, he said, "Positively no! Strings? What could I do with strings that hasn't been done wonderfully for hundreds of years?"

Even though most critics wrote well of the

concert, they felt Duke was starting to lose his spark, his ability to excite an audience.

A month later, several of his top players, feeling that the end was near, bailed. Headliners Johnny Hodges and trombonist Lawrence Brown took Sonny Greer with them and formed their own small group. Greer was the last of the Washingtonians. They did some recording under Norman Ganz, who'd been working with Duke since 1941 and "Jump For Joy" in Los Angeles. Ganz had been instrumental in booking Ellington's tours after Irving Mills left in 1940, and had been a good friend and business associate.

The news hit Duke like a bolt of lightening, and things seemed to have finally come to an end. But Duke was not one to look back and hang on to the past. To him, his best number was the one he was composing at the moment. The best band was the one he was standing in front of. The best players were the ones he was currently developing. He was a consummate opportunist, and he was determined to keep his band alive. Not just to make money, but because he couldn't write music without his band. In fact, he used to say, "My instrument is my band." Although he played the piano, he really played the entire band as if it were an extension of his mind. He needed a

Ellington and Irving Mills. Mills managed Ellington and his band for years but they parted in 1940. However, Mills continued to collect royalities on Duke's compositions until 1960.

group of good musicians so he could hear what his melodies and harmonies sounded like.

Drastic times meant drastic action, and Duke met the challenge by doing something he'd never done before, hiring away leading musicians from other bands. He grabbed trumpeter and band leader Harry James' three leading players, offering them more money and heaping flattering compliments on them like they'd never heard before. And Ellington was a grand charmer, and a wicked street fighter when he had to be.

Although he'd always worked under the no poaching agreement with other band leaders, this was different; he was fighting for his survival. He nabbed saxophonist Willie Smith; drummer Louis Bellson; and, on the trombone, Juan Tizol, marking his return to Ellington.

The move was significant for another reason. It marked the first time Duke hired a white musician, Louis Bellson, as a full time member.

Duke had luckily hired a star tenor saxophonist before the break up. A few months earlier, Paul Gonsalves had been offered to fill the hole left by Ben Webster. It would still be a while, however, before Gonsalves would grow into the part and establish his own style. He could let loose fast solos, one after the other with incredible ease and fluidity, then play a warm ballad with a breathy, rich tone. He'd worked with both Count Basie and Dizzy Gillespie, but he'd always been an admirer of Duke Ellington. He knew every Webster solo by heart. He was a shy and almost missed his chance to meet Ellington because he was too nervous to go up and shake his hand. While Duke was doing a show at Charlie Parker's Birdland, which had just opened up, Gonsalves waited until the last moment to meet his idol.

Pleased with the young man and his playing, Duke told him to come to the office the next day. Duke's band was in need of a tenor saxophonist and Gonsalves had the job if he wanted it. Just to be in the band was success enough for Gonsalves. When he started learning the sax, his boyhood dream was to play with Duke Ellington.

Unfortunately, he arrived at one of the lowest ebbs of Duke's career.

While the aggressive move didn't pull Duke out of troubled times, it showed that he was committed to keeping his orchestra together, no matter what the cost. Of all the traits that helped Duke become a success, it was tenacity and determination that helped the most. When it came to music, nothing got in the way. Even his marriage took a backseat to the music, leading to the separation in the early 30s. Several girlfriends followed, including, Mildred Dixon in the 30s, and Beatrice Ellis, with whom he lived in New York for over 30 years, and was the closest thing to a wife he ever had. Both Dixon and Ellis were dancers Duke met while performing at the Cotton Club, and quite extraordinary beauties. Even though Duke lived with Beatrice Ellis, and introduced her as Evie Ellington to associates, she was rarely seen in public with him, and never accompanied him on his tours.

During the next five years, Ellington's popularity continued to decline, and so did the band. He soon lost Bellson and Willie Smith, both replaced with lesser talented players. Occasionally, however, the band could rally itself and give a spirited performance. Another performance of "New World A-Comin'" and "Harlem" was extremely well received, but such moments were becoming increasingly rarer.

By 1955, the best gig Duke could get was playing mood music at a water park. Duke couldn't lead his own band. He would play a piano solo, then the house conductor would take over and he could go home if he wanted to. The critics were especially severe, claiming that Duke was now merely a footnote to the history of jazz.

Even at his darkest hour, Duke continued to work furiously as if he were still on top. Perhaps that would be his biggest reason for success. No matter how bad things got, he never dwelt on them, but continued to look at what he was about to do. His comment about playing for the "Aquacades," was that at least he got home early, and was able to spend some time writing a play, "Man with Four Sides," and "Night Creature," for a radio orchestra, which was to be played at Carnegie Hall by Duke's band. Duke's relationship with record companies had become so terrible that it would take eight years to get "Night Creature" released on an album.

Duke persisted, and by a lucky turn of events, he was able to get Johnny Hodges, whose band had broken up while Duke was doing the water show. He also hired a top drummer, Sam Woodyard. With the two new musicians, Duke was able to get a deal with Capitol for a "best of" record "Historically Speaking, the Duke." It was a boost for the band because it was the best music they'd played for years, and they knew it. They still needed to convince a significant audience.

By the middle of the 50s, jazz had taken another turn. The turbulent sounds of bebop

At one point, in the 1950s, Ellington was so out of favor that he was reduced to playing mood music at a water park. Because of union regulations he couldn't lead his own band!

He would play a piano solo, then the house conductor would take over and he could go home if he wanted to. The critics were especially severe, predicting that his career was finished.

and Dixieland had given way to a softer, more moody trend called "cool jazz," that has now been refined into modern jazz. It is this style of music that most people associate with jazz. It's the sound of the finger-snapping beatniks.

Outdoor jazz festivals were to become the mega-musical events of the 50s. It was where all the different forms of jazz got together: Dixieland, New Orleans style, big band, bebop, and modern. It was like a living anthology of the history of jazz. Everyone was there, from record company executives to promoters, star musicians, magazine reviewers, music publishers, newspaper columnists, photographers, and, of course, a battery of the most zealous jazz fans from across the country.

Duke had been invited to represent the big bands, but they didn't want to headline him because he no longer had drawing power. And sadly, they were right. Duke was determined to change that, however. He knew that no matter how his band was billed, he had to make a good showing at Newport.

His back was against the wall.

About the same time, Duke switched from Capital to sign up again with Columbia Records, and happened to team up with a very progressive minded producer, Irving Townsend.

Columbia wanted to record Duke live at Newport, and just before going on, he met with Townsend to discuss future deals. Duke insisted on being paid up front so he could meet his payroll, and he'd take his personal fees from the publishing. He also wanted to do new music for future albums.

Townsend agreed to the deal, and Duke went onstage where his band was already playing "Take The A Train." Unfortunately, they were four players short, not a good sign for a band that was supposed to be on a come back.

He played a few numbers and was followed by other starring acts, including Teddy Wilson, Anita O'Day, and Chico Hamilton. The promoters wouldn't put Duke back on until around midnight. After a few rousing performances, the festival seemed to naturally peak out, and the crowd of 10,000 began to leave. Duke complained to the festival promotion," What are we, the animal act?" He felt betrayed that he was given the worst slot of the evening to stage a comeback performance.

The audience were already filing out through the gates when Duke Ellington got back on stage. He opened with his recent work, "Newport Jazz Festival Suite," and played a couple more numbers, and the audience was, for the most part, polite, but many continued to leave because of the late hour.

After four numbers, Duke was left with his closing act, and he knew that this was his last chance to excite the crowd. He told Paul Gonsalves, his solo tenor saxophonist, to take as many choruses as he wanted, but Gonsalves was a keen performer by now. He knew how to read a crowd, and play just the right amount to build up excitement, then give it back to the band for the finale. It would usually fall between five to seven, if the crowd was especially receptive.

Right from the start of "Diminuendo and Crescendo in Blue," the sound was so exotic, so compelling that people started to take notice. When Paul Gonsalves started in on his solo, supported rhythmically with the bass and the drummer, people in the aisles who had turned backs to the stage to leave, began to stop and listen. A few more bars, and it was obvious that something unexpected was shaping up on the stage. It was not polished, not canned; it was something spontaneous and mysterious. No one was leaving any longer. They were all stopped, turned to the stage and began to snap their fingers with the music. Paul Gonsalves continued to rip through his solo choruses, making them seem effortless. It was a stunning contrast between animalistic

By the 1950s it was common for white singers to appear with black jazz bands. June Christy was the "girl singer" with Nat King Cole. The only white to sing for Duke was Alice Babs.

fervor and a prayer. The finger snapping turned into hand clapping as Gonsalves kept it up. Even another drummer stood in the pit and tapped along with Gonsalves by pounding a rolled up newspapers on the side of the stage, and shouting encouragement. Those who'd remained seated, got to their feet and clapped along. They started to scream, "More, more!" The crowd of nearly 10,000 was electrified and unified. People were dancing in the aisles, and the festival organizers began to fear the crowd might riot at any moment. One even asked Duke to tell Gonsalves to stop, but Duke reproved him, and let Gonsalves continue. Sudden, as the crowd worked to a climax, the band burst in with Duke taking a brief piano solo before Cat Anderson closed the show with his high-pitched trumpeting.

The crowd had become so electrified that instead of wanting to leave, they demanded more encores. Duke played four, ending well after one o'clock in the morning.

It all got recorded by the engineers from Columbia.

Virtually overnight, after nearly 10 years of decline, Duke Ellington was sitting on top of the world of jazz. The buzz throughout the music industry was his electrifying performance at Newport. Within two weeks, Duke

Ellington made the cover of "Time" magazine.

Suddenly there was an explosion of new bookings at colleges, clubs, and concert halls. Where Columbia may have been sluggish in recording new pieces, they actively pushed up recording dates to get new albums out. The publicity created a renewed interest in Duke Ellington. Older recordings were reissued on longer playing albums, and students of jazz could trace the development of his music. Many were surprised to realize just how far reaching his influence on the course of jazz had been. The golden years of the 40s was rediscovered through the records. It caused many to take another look at his more recent concerts and extended works, realizing just how unique and subtle they were. Indeed, Duke had never limited himself to the popular constraints of a trend, but had always tried to express his emotions and imagination the best he could.

As Duke Ellington approached his 60th birthday, he composed and performed with the energy and enthusiasm of a 20 year old. At an age when many start thinking of retiring, he was getting ready to embark on his most prolific and creative period yet. From age 60 to his death, more than a decade later, Duke was going to reach yet another musical peak.

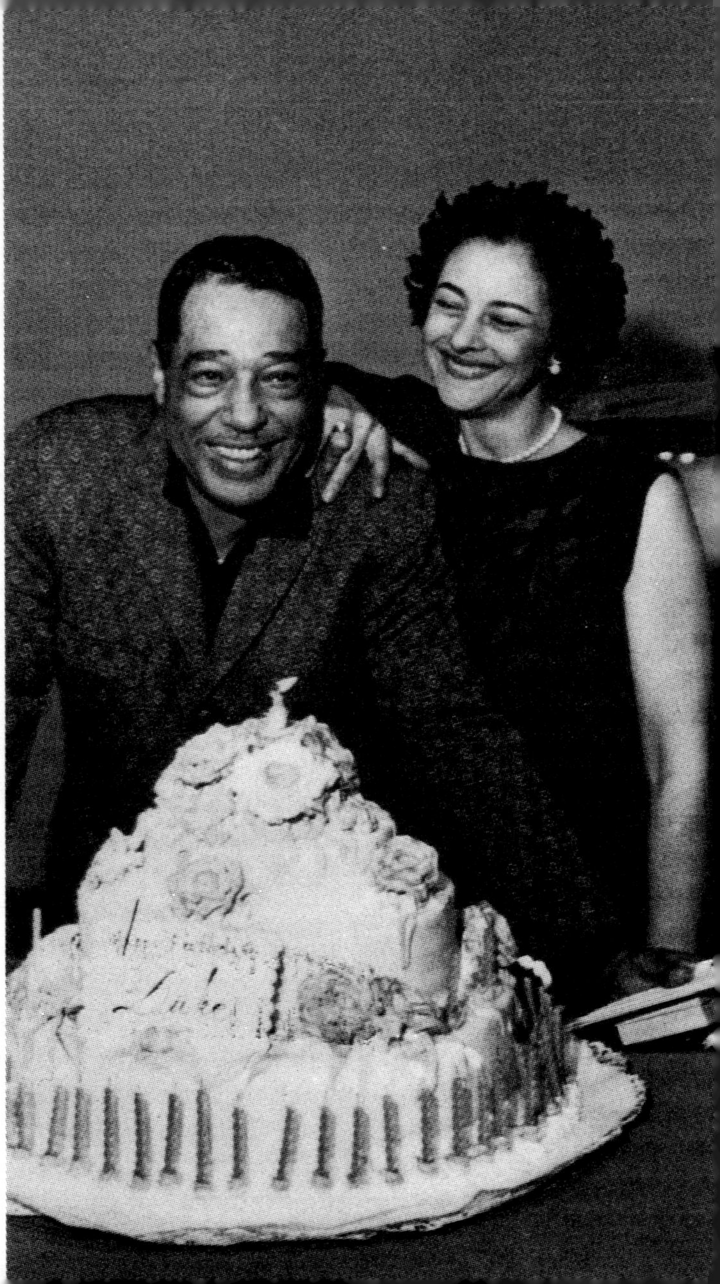

Chapter Eight

Ambassador of Music

FEW ARTISTS BLOSSOM IN their later years the way Duke Ellington did. He was determined to do his own music, and break away from all confinements of category, even if it meant putting out an album knowing it was going to lose money. His sacred concerts were a huge drain on his own resources, but he was committed to doing the best he could. He'd been through the worst and survived. Previous works had received tepid reviews only to be reversed years later when the times (and critics) changed, so he didn't particularly care what anyone thought about his music,

---

Duke Ellington and longtime companion Evie Ellis celebrate his 65th birthday on April 29, 1964. Although he spent 35 years with Evie, he never divorced his wife, Edna Thompson.

so long as he liked it personally.

The decision was a sound one for Duke because as he was preparing for his most artistically successful period, the nation's youngsters were turning from jazz to a new trend in music, a variation of rhythm and blues that would be called rock and roll.

Duke never attempted to write rock and roll. Not that he didn't like the music, he said it was out of character for him.

Ironically, rock and roll actually helped Duke Ellington's artistic success during the 60s. With the new music taking the heat as being the current irreverent and vulgar style in music, jazz had now been "legitimized" in America as a new music form, as it had been decades previously in Europe.

Ellington was no longer considered popular music; he had made it into the ranks of the artists. Serious compositions would dominate his attention for the rest of his life.

His first original composition after the Newport Festival, "A Drum is a Woman," premiered on color television. It had been an idea suggested by a conversation with Orson Welles in 1941: the history of jazz from its African roots up to the present told through music and dance. Despite its grand scale, the work never created the sensation Ellington had hoped for.

"Such Sweet Thunder," however, did create quite a stir. It also came out in 1957, and was inspired by Shakespeare's plays. Ellington and Billy Strayhorn wrote a series of numbers that were portraits of Lady Macbeth, Hamlet, Iago, Romeo and Juliet, Henry V, Puck, among others. Writer Derek Jewell commented, "There was wit, lush beauty, and evocative invention in every one of these portraits."

Also in 1957, he recorded "Royal Ancestry," a three-part portrait of the great singer Ella Fitzgerald, with whom he had worked, and greatly admired. He would make two tours in the 60s with her, one to Europe and another to the Virgin Islands.

When he was invited to Monterey, he based another suite on John Steinbeck's books "Cannery Row" and "Sweet Thursday." He called it "Suite Thursday." After trying it out on the crowd, and modifying a few of the rough sections, Ellington recorded it a few weeks later, and it was released with much praise from both public and critics alike.

The higher profile once again made Duke attractive to Hollywood, and Otto Preminger hired him to do the music score for "Anatomy of a Murder," which starred James Stewart. Duke even played the piano in one scene. It was his first complete movie score.

He went to Paris in 1960 to do "Paris Blues." which starred Paul Newman and Sidney Poitier. Duke also wrote music for a classic French play that hadn't been staged since 1709. In 1966, he was also hired to do music for "Assault on the Queen," but apparently he didn't get along with the director, and much of his music got cut. After screening the movie, the director asked Duke what he thought. "I think it's the best western I've ever seen," Duke said to the director who didn't know if he was really serious or insulting him.

In 1958, he visited England again. The highlight was a festival of arts in Leeds, which was organized by Queen Elizabeth II's cousin. Many in the Royal Family were still ardent Ellington fans, and it was only natural they'd invite him as one of the headliners. Although Queen Elizabeth couldn't make the concert, Princess Margaret did. Duke had written a number especially for her, "Princess Blue." Later, when he had the occasion to meet the Queen, he promised to write her a special suite, as he'd done for Princess Margaret.

During the next year, at his own expense, he recorded the "Queen's Suite," pressed only one record, which he sent to Buckingham Palace for the Queen's personal enjoyment.

The record was never released to the general public while Duke was alive, but his son, Mercer, issued a version a few years after his death, showing just how beautiful and majestic it was.

Just before Duke left Paris during his 1960 visit, he was invited to perform at the Palais de la Defense for a special Christmas Eve mass. He played before a crowd of 100,000, and they were quite moved by his invigorating music. It was the first time Duke played for an event with a religious context, and was delighted with the results.

Mahalia Jackson, the great gospel singer, so eloquently described Ellington's unique stature during the 60s. She was known for always refusing to sing in night clubs or working with jazz groups. When she recorded with Duke Ellington for his "Black, Brown and Beige" record in 1958, she answered her critics with: "Duke Ellington's orchestra isn't a jazz band; it's a sacred institution."

By 1963, he was so busy he would fly between Ontario, Canada, where he was doing music for a Shakespeare play; and Chicago, where he was staging a play.

Then he would return to New York, where he worked with choreographers. Between all that, he'd fly to wherever the band was doing a one-nighter, do a performance and hop a plane to either Chicago, New York or Ontario the next morning.

The play in Chicago was part of an arts festival to commemorate the 100th anniversary of the Emancipation Proclamation, and had been supported strongly by John F. Kennedy, then the president of the United States. The production, "My People," was an enormous success, showing that Ellington still had a handle on his visual talents, creating both dance and lighting effects that created spectacular results for the audience.

The race situation throughout the country was heating up as blacks and human rights activists of all ethnic groups staged demonstrations, rallies, marches, and parades in support of civil rights. There'd already been several summer riots, and several marches that could have broken into full out riots had the police tried to interfere. Martin Luther King Jr. was leading his famous boycott in the south when Duke Ellington wrote a tribute to his struggle which was included in "My People". The biblical walls of Jericho were symbolized by white police with firehoses and guard dogs savagely attacking black civil rights activists. It was an arousing blend of song, dance, theater, and social criticism.

In the fall, he was invited by the State Department to go on a world tour that took him to such exotic places as Syria, Jerusalem, Beirut, Kuwait, Iraq, Afghanistan, India, Pakistan, and Ceylon.

During the tour, he not only gave concerts, but lectures for students and musicians interested in jazz. Duke's energy was phenomenal. Often, when the band would land at an airport, the weary, sleepy travelers would all head directly to the hotel and dive bomb into the beds to rest before the next concert.

Not Duke, who was the oldest in the group. He would be whisked off to the airport to do radio and television interviews, meet with journalists, or be ushered off to greet government officials and members of the various royal families in the different countries he visited. When he got to India, he fell sick, and had to spend four days in the hospital recuperating from the flu. His friend and personal physician, Arthur Logan, flew from America to lend a helping hand, although he was well cared for by an Indian doctor, who was also a great fan of Ellington's music. When Duke went to visit him, the doctor asked him how long before his next concert.

"An hour," Duke replied.

"You don't have a temperature now, so it's

okay to do the concert, but I'll check you later to make sure you're all right."

During the performance, the doctor sat in the front row, and thoroughly enjoyed the performance. The minute it was over, he went back stage, checked Duke's temperature, and said, "You have a fever now. We have to take you to the hospital."

Duke and his entourage learned of President Kennedy's assassination while they were in Turkey, sending a chill through the group and the country, which had been a strong supporter of Kennedy during the Cuban missile crisis.

While the tour ended on a sad note, it was a great success, and opened up other such world tours sponsored by the State Department. They went to the Orient in 1964, and the Virgin Islands in 1965. Africa in 1966, and, in 1968 they toured through South and Central America, starting in Argentina and ending in Mexico City, where the band played a suite Duke had been writing during his travels. In 1969, he visited Eastern Europe, and in 1971, he went to the Soviet Union.

The tours also supplied Ellington and Strayhorn with inspiration for suites. While Duke claimed to be the world's worst tourist, and confessed in his autobiography that he didn't actually "see" the Taj Mahal when he was in India, Billy Strayhorn was enraptured with sight seeing, rummaging through bazaars and markets. It was Strayhorn who soaked up the local scenery, flavors, people and music, and worked his impressions into the suites he and Duke composed.

After Strayhorn's death in 1967, Duke seemed to gear up his writing even more intensely in honor of his collaborator and close friend.

Though it was never planned, Duke Ellington had become "a de facto" ambassador to the world for jazz.

During the tours throughout the 60s, they were constantly asked by reporters about the racial situation currently going on in the United States. Like a true diplomat, Duke was able to speak his mind and yet not offend anyone. He once had to remind a reporter in India that Martin Luther King Jr., while fighting for rights of poverty stricken blacks, lived, himself, an affluent lifestyle, with a chauffeur-driven Cadillac and often police escorts wherever he went. A lifestyle that only the very rich in India enjoyed, but in America, it was considered middle class, even for blacks.

The African tour, which culminated with the

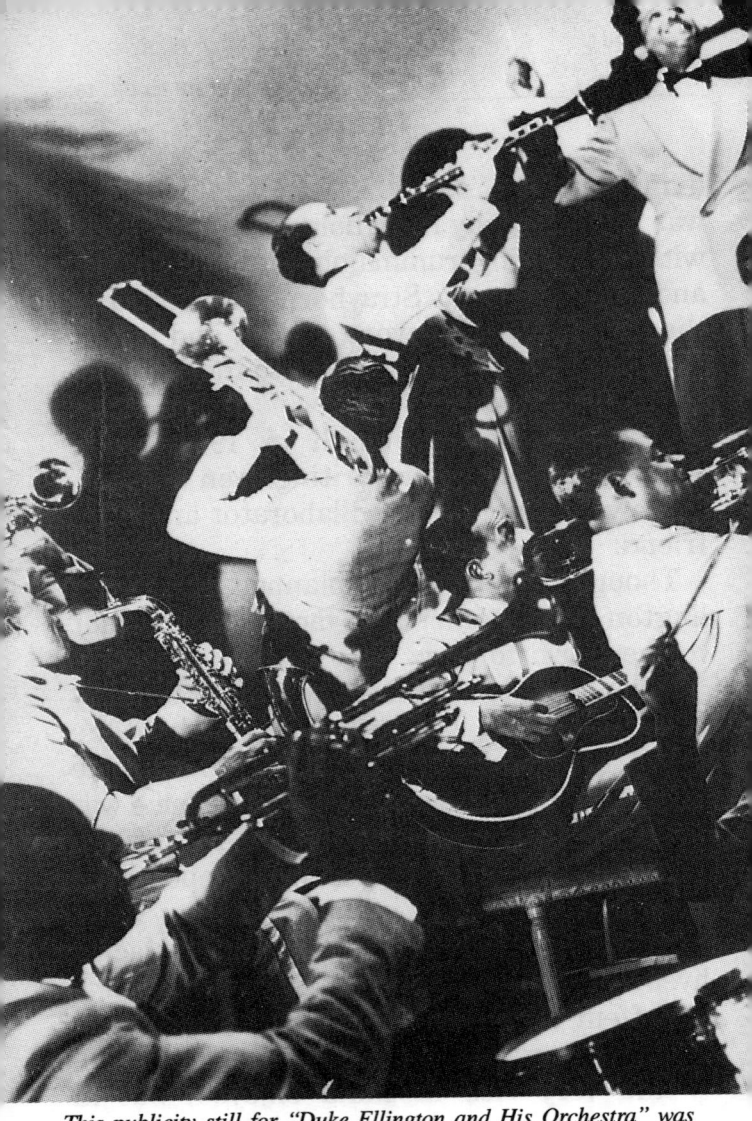

This publicity still for "Duke Ellington and His Orchestra" was released by the William Morris Agency in the late 1950s, after he'd created a sensation at the the Newport Jazz Festival.

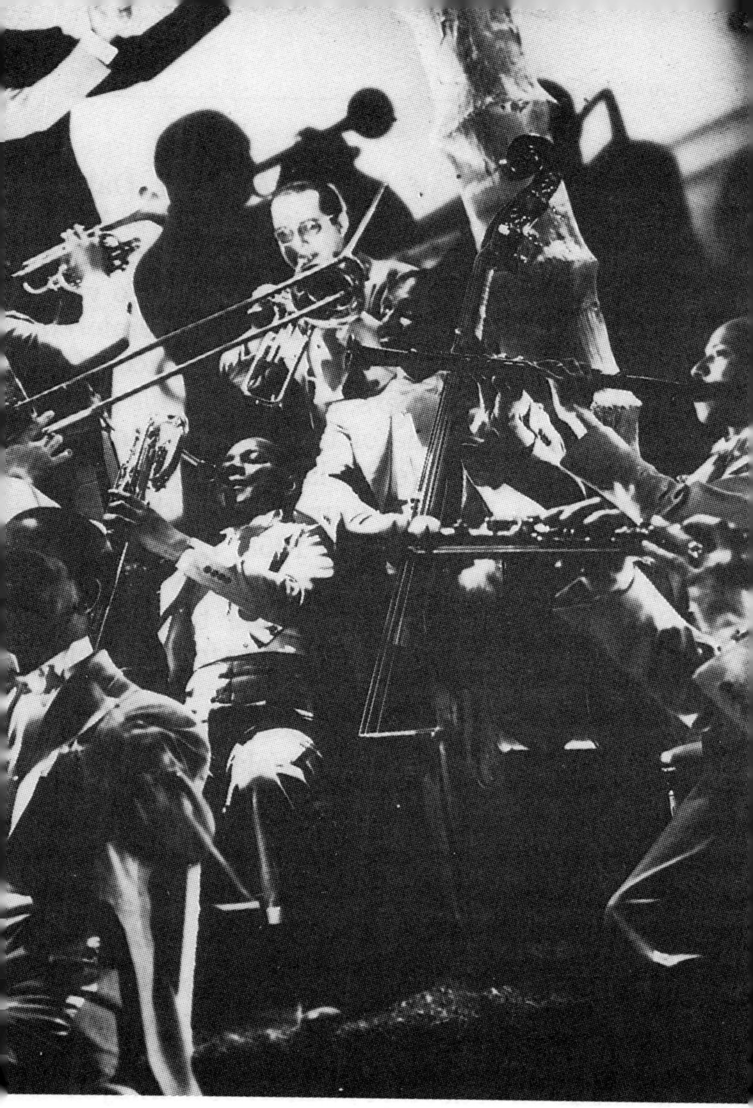

World Festival of Negro Arts in Dakar, Senegal, was a special favorite of Duke's. After over four decades of performing music based on African roots, he was finally able to visit the continent for the first time. He premiered his "La Plus Belle Africaine." Being accepted by his African brothers, and sharing his music with them, was one of the most moving experiences of his life, he later said.

The 1971 Russian tour was another high point for two reasons. In 1958, Duke and all black musicians had been passed over by the State Department for a similar tour. Benny Goodman had assembled a group for the event, and no blacks were invited.

He was met at the airport by a Russian marching band playing Dixieland style jazz, with sliding trombones, wailing clarinets and screaming trumpets. It was quite an unexpected event, to say the least.

Duke was delighted to discover that a museum in Leningrad had over eighteen hundred paintings from the impressionist, post-Impressionists, and even a pre-Cubistic Picasso. While Duke never pursued his natural talent as an artist and painter, he'd always remained an art fan.

In Kiev, he was startled by the enormous police force that showed up. When he inquired why there were so many, he was told they were members of the police band, and they all just wanted to see Duke Ellington.

Duke was also impressed with the polite yet tenacious appreciation Russians had for him during the concerts. Not a single person would leave or even stand up before the concert was finished, but they often demanded encore after encore, often going hours beyond the scheduled time.

The Russian tour was just the beginning of a longer tour, which lasted over three months. After five weeks in the Soviet Union, he spent five more in Europe, performing in a different city every night, and ending up in Scandinavia. From the cold north he went straight to sunny Rio de Janerio. Unlike the 1968 Latin American tour, this was more leisurely, and he was able to spend more time soaking up the environment and local music.

The next year, another tour had him back in the Orient for another burst of flash appearances.

At the time, Duke was 71 years old, and he was still performing and composing at an unbelievable intensity.

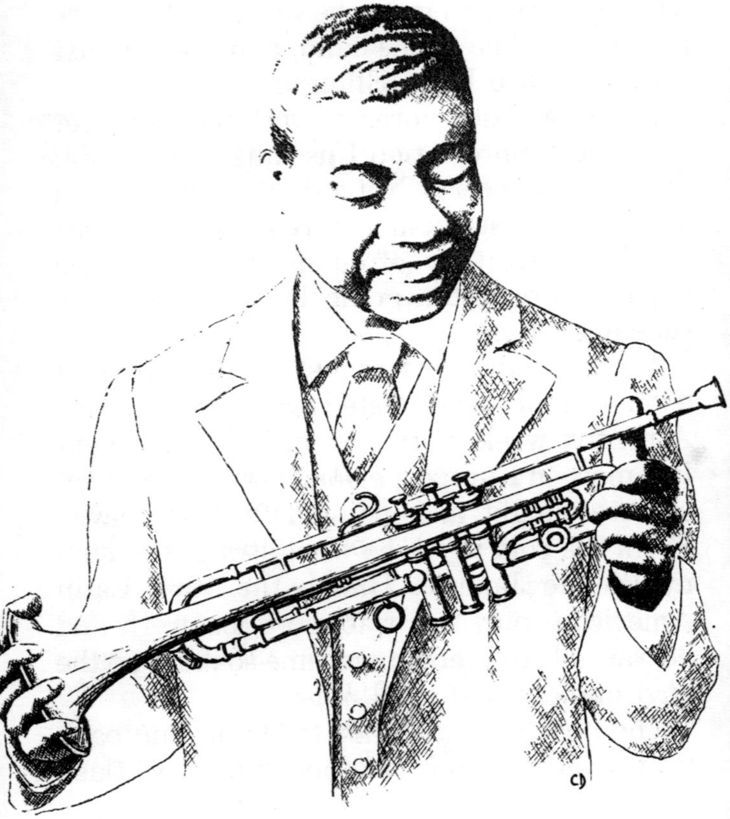
CD

Chapter Nine

Diminuendo

IN ADDITION TO THE world tours, Duke Ellington continued to perform one-night shows all across the country, and made annual appearances at many outdoor jazz festivals in the States. He had a particularly good showing in 1970 in New Orleans, where he presented his "New Orleans Suite" as a tribute to Johnny Hodges who'd just passed away.

With other close friends, long-time bandmembers and musicians passing away—Louis Armstrong and Willie "The Lion" Smith also died in 1970—it is little wonder Ellington con-

The great Louis Armstrong. While Ellington and Armstrong greatly admired each other, and appeared "unofficially" together on stage on a few special occasions, they never joined forces.

tinued to compose at a frantic pace, focusing his attention on completing his final Sacred Concert.

The three Sacred Concerts were perhaps Ellington's most precious and self-expressive works, although not his most memorable. Many of the numbers could have easily been performed successfully in a dance hall or night club. They were unique in that they marked a point when jazz was "able" to be played in a place of religious worship, and be appreciated as one man's way of praising his God.

When an episcopalian priest asked him to perform at Grace Cathedral in San Francisco, he decided to do a spiritual concert specially written for the occasion rather than just perform a medley of some of his favorite songs. He didn't set a traditional service to music, nor did he adapt black gospel music. He wanted to do it his own way.

Between appearances and finding time when he could, he started jotting down notes and ideas for his first sacred concert, which was finally premiered in September of 1965. It was something of a miracle just to see Johnny Hodges, Harry Carney and Paul Gonsalves, all on saxes, in a place of worship, belting out their evocative reed sounds while a choir sang in the background and dancers moved in the foreground. As bizarre a mix it was in a religious context, it was greatly received.

He did another performance a few months later at the Presbyterian Church in New York City, which had been set up by a pastor who worked with jazz musicians in New York, John Gensel. He'd been a fan since 1932, and was the creator of the Duke Ellington Jazz Society in the 50s. He said of Duke's sudden interest in religious music, "You could see that this was the thing he loved to do most. And he did it his own way, without saying, 'I'm the preacher.'"

The "Second Sacred Concert" was also presented in New York, at the Cathedral Church of St. John the Divine. One of the largest cathedrals in the world, it seated over 2,000. It was as successful as the first one, and he received requests from all over the world to perform it, which he did nearly 50 times.

As Duke started working on his third and final sacred concert, it was becoming obvious that something was wrong. Near the end of 1972, he was complaining of chronic sickness, and he was sent to the hospital for tests. X-rays revealed lung cancer. As 1973 progressed, he set to work finishing the "Third Sacred

Concert," which was to premiere in the fall at Westminster Abbey, in London, kicking off another European/African tour.

On the flight over to London, Mercer, who had been managing the band since 1964, figured out something was wrong. His pace was off, and he just didn't have the strength he usually displayed just prior to a performance. Duke worked best under pressure, and knew just how much he could get done in time for opening night.

Despite his weak condition, the concert went well, with the exception of Paul Gonsalves collapsing in the middle of a rehearsal and having to be rushed to a hospital. Duke did have to take a ten minute rest while Ella Fitzgerald and the band were left on their own.

Gonsalves caught up with the band in Germany, where they continued the tour. They played at various sites in Sweden, Germany, Holland, Yugoslavia, France, Belgium, Ethiopia and Zambia, then back to England and Ireland.

Just before a command performance before Queen Elizabeth II word of Dr. Arthur Logan's death arrived, but Duke wasn't told until after the concert.

When he finally heard, Duke went into another depression. Just before leaving for the tour, he and Logan had discussed various medical options for Duke's condition, and he felt that when he returned, they'd be able to find a way out of it.

He finished the tour with a few more appearances in Ireland and England, then returned to the States. He performed the "Third Sacred Concert" for the second and last time at a church in Harlem. Even in his weakened condition, he set out on the road again for a tour of the Midwest. It was as Mercer said, "He just refused to admit that he was sick. Even then, there wasn't much that could have been done for him either, so as long as he was capable of leading the band, he did."

The list of awards and honors Duke received throughout his life is a vast and impressive one. At the top of the list, of course, were the two medals he received at the white house: President's Gold Medal, presented by Lyndon B. Johnson; and the Presidential Medal of Freedom, presented by Richard M. Nixon. France awarded him with the Legion of Honor, and Ethiopia with the Emperor's Star. Seven states gave him special recognition, and several even declared a Duke Ellington day.

He won just about every music award given, over a dozen honorary Doctor of Music degrees from universities, was given life-time membership into the American Federation of Musicians, Academy of Arts and Sciences, Royal Swedish Academy of Music, the Songwriters' Hall of fame (he was the 5th member to be inducted), to name just a few. He was even appointed honorary Marshall of Dodge City. He placed at the top of magazine polls almost every year since 1945, except for the mid 50s, and dominated "Down Beat," "Jazz Magazine," "Esquire," and "Playboy" polls during the 60s. The republics of Togoland and Chad commemorated Duke Ellington with a postage stamp.

There was one award that did get away from him, the Pulitzer Prize. Even though the music jury had unanimously nominated Duke Ellington in 1965, the Pulitzer board rejected it.

The rejection caused a major uproar in the music world, many citing, with good cause, that racial prejudice was the sole reason not to give him a special citation in music. Two prominent members of the Pulitzer music committee quit in protest.

In 1964, he brought his son, Mercer, into the band as its manager and to hold a seat down in the trumpet section. Their relationship was a strange one at best, but frankly, he had not been a very good father to his son. In Mercer's

Mercer Ellington, Duke's son. However, once Mercer let his hair turned gray, Duke would sometimes seriously introduce him as "my father." Duke Ellington had a problem with aging.

autobiography he said that his father resented him for not being a girl. "He wanted a daughter. It was like Ellington to buck the traditions of the time. When everyone else wanted a son, Ellington wanted a daughter."

While he lavished gifts on his sister, Ruth—a mink coat on her 16th birthday, a Cadillac later on and trips to Europe—Mercer was given only customary gifts. Duke encouraged him to get into music, although he had started playing some successful semi-pro football, and had a promising career ahead of him. He received a scholarship to study engineering, but Duke preferred he go to Juillard, even though Duke resented formal music education. When Mercer started his own band, Duke lent a helping hand, but only to a degree. He refused to have "two" Ellingtons star on Broadway. He'd seen what had happened to Cab Calloway when his brother started making a big name for himself. It wiped him out.

Even as manager, Mercer rode with the musicians while Duke usually traveled separately. Later on, when Mercer started growing gray hair, he introduced his son as his father, Mercer Ellington. It was no sly joke. Duke was afraid of growing old, and seeing his son growing gray hair terrified him. He often shunned people who reminded him of how old he'd become. He once refused to talk to a middle-aged lady who'd come up to him in the Cotton Club to say hello because he'd had a romantic liaison with her years before, when she was still a young, attractive woman. Yet, despite the resentment, Duke felt close to his son, and was happy that the family was at least working together.

Trying to understand Duke Ellington's character, and what drove him so hard during his last years is not an easy task. He was so many things to so many different people. As Rex Stewart so aptly put it, describing how Ellington changed over the years, "He grows grander but more introspective. He has apparently learned to give more of himself in public but less in private." Even as late as 1968, he called such long time players as Cootie Williams and Harry Carney by their full names.

Duke's work day was reversed from the norm. He worked nights, usually after a concert or on the way to another gig. Normally, he got to bed around 9 a.m., slept to around 2 or 3, but didn't get out of bed. He had a habit of making phone calls while still moving as little as possible, usually with a towel around his head and a robe on.

Once he fell to sleep, he was dead to the

world, a trait that has been the subject of countless anecdotes by band members and road managers, who had the responsibilities of rousing him out of his incredible slumber. One road manager later said that he'd grown so weary of trying to wake up Duke that he once left him on a train that was shunted off into a siding five miles from the depot in Tacoma, Washington, to teach him a lesson. The walk back didn't faze him, and he continued to sleep as deeply as ever.

Another time, Ellington stumbled sleepily from a train, got into a line of men climbing onto a bus, and found himself sitting with hardened criminals on their way to the San Quentin prison. The road manager, who had to chase him down in a car, found it almost impossible to convince the dubious bus driver that Duke Ellington was not a prisoner.

In speech, Duke always enjoyed the sound of words and clever turns to compliment a person, especially women. When a certain phrase was especially effective, he'd continue to use it on everyone he met, driving the band nuts after a few years. He once exclaimed after a performance, "We love you madly," and they responded with a huge applause. Since then, the phrase became a pat idiom of Duke's concerts. His use of language was greatly enhanced after meeting Billy Strayhorn, who was well educated and extremely eloquent.

Despite his charm and easy way with women, Mercer later wrote, "Ellington actually disliked many women. It was a love-hate relationship." Even though he deeply cared for Evie, she was often left alone and Duke would meet social engagements, such as his 70th birthday party at the White House, accompanied with his sister, Ruth, not Evie. Evie, in fact, was only very rarely seen with Duke in public, and had become quite lonely in her latter life as Duke's tours became longer and his commitments kept him on the road.

By the beginning of 1974, while the band was in Illinois, Duke Ellington collapsed once again and was hospitalized. Now he was too weak to continue, and after the tour, the Duke Ellington Orchestra was suspended, and not reunited until Mercer took it to Bermuda the day after Duke's death.

As Duke was being examined, one of the doctors confided in Mercer, "You know if he goes into a hospital he isn't coming out."

"I know," Mercer said.

"Does he know that," the doctor asked Mercer.

"Yes."

Even in the hospital, with daily visits from

friends and relatives and the remaining musicians, Duke continued to work. He discussed how to record the "Third Sacred Concert" with Mercer, then decided on judicial editing of what had been recorded at Westminster Abbey.

Mercer had brought in an electric piano, which Duke doodled on, tinkering with melodies and harmonies, in between jotting notes.

Evie Ellington (Beatrice Ellis), the woman who had been more a wife to Duke than anyone else, found out she, too, had cancer, and was soon hospitalized herself. Near the middle of May, Paul Gonsalves passed away while visiting friends in London. While his relationship with Duke had been a rocky one, Duke had always been fond of the quiet yet erratic young man, whose saxophone style was one of the most eloquent he'd ever heard. Within days, another band member, Tyree Glenn, a trombonist who joined the band in 1947, passed away.

During the early hours on May 24, 1974, Duke Ellington quietly passed away.

The bodies of Duke Ellington, Paul Gonsalves and Tyree Glenn, were laid out together in a funeral home, signifying the passing of an era. Already gone were Bubber Miley, Rex

The Duke in 1974. He worked up to the very end. Mercer has indicated that Duke felt as long as he was working, life would go on and things would remain the same.

Stewart, Artie Whetsol, Joe Nanton, Otto Hardwick, Johnny Hodges, Ben Webster, Freddy Guy, Jimmy Blanton, and Oscar Pettiford. Soon after, as if heeding a call, Harry Carney passed away, and, a year later, so did Beatrice "Evie" Ellis.

The funeral at Cathedral of St. John the Divine drew a huge crowd inside and thousands were outside who couldn't get in. Many shops in Harlem closed to mourn Ellington. The radio played his most memorable songs, and eulogies came from everywhere. Jazz critic, Ralph Gleason, said Duke was "the greatest composer this American society has produced." Alister Cooke ended his comments by applying to Duke what John O'Hara had said about George Gershwin, "Duke Ellington died last week. I don't have to believe it if I don't want to." Stanley Dance, who gave the eulogy at the service, said Duke "was loved throughout the whole world, at all levels of society, by Frenchmen and Germans, by English and Irish, by Arabs and Jews, by Indians and Pakistanis, by atheists and devout Catholics, and by communists and fascists alike."

President Nixon said, "The wit, taste, intelligence, and elegance that Duke Ellington brought to his music has made him, in the eyes of millions of people both here and abroad, America's foremost composer. His memory will live for generations..."

Fortunately Duke Ellington began his compositions about the same time recording devices were invented, enabling future generations to trace his development through his actual playing, not his writing. He had, after all, learned his craft first by listening and playing it live, and then setting it to paper after he'd polished a song with his band.

It was Duke Ellington who showed the way to bridge jazz into the mainstream of music. He added the elegance and sophistication, but managed to keep the raw, primitive power and flavors. Duke always hated the term "jazz" because it was too restrictive. He always said he did music that sprung from African roots that had been adapted through years of slavery and repression in America, which included jazz but could also be an opera, a ballad, a ballet, a musical, or a religious concert, all of which Duke Ellington composed and performed at one time or another.

INDEX

Alcohol, problems with, 93–95, 143
Apollo Bar, 139, 141
Barron's, 47, 50
Battle of the Bands, 106–107
Bebop, 136
"Black and Tan Fantasy," 71–72, 107
"Black, Brown, and Beige," 129–132
Blanton, Jimmy, 122–123, 126
"Blue Belles of Harlem," 54
Capone, Al, 67
Carnegie Hall, 131–132
Carney, Harry, 57, 96, 102, 174, 181, 186
Chicago Theater, 97
Cool jazz, 152
Cotton Club, 60–61, 64, 68, 76, 148, 181
Dance, Stanley, 11, 92, 186
Diamond, Renee and Leslie, 11, 84, 142
Dixieland jazz, 136
"East St. Louis Toodle-oo," 56
Eisenhower, Dwight D., 18
Ellington, Daisy Kennedy (mother of Duke Ellington), 18, 22
illness and death, 100–101
Ellington, Edna, (wife of Duke Ellington), 11, 34, 51–53
Ellington, Edward Kennedy "Duke"
abstinence, 94
acting experience, 128
appearance, cover "Time" magazine, 157
attitude toward critics, 159–160
autobiography, 10
awards, 11–12, 16, 30, 88, 177–178
beliefs, 10, 131
biographer, *see* Dance, Stanley
birth, 21
birth of son, 36
birthday party, 70th, 9
birthday party, Sweden, 112
breakup of marriage, 51–52
college scholarship, 30
commission for concert, 54
composing style, 71–72, 98, 181
concerts, 129–135, 143, 161, 174–176
Cotton Club audition, 61, 64
critical acclaim, 85
death, 184
death of parents, 101–102
decline in popularity, 148–149
development of musical style, 54
early employment, 26–34, 36
education, 27, 30
family background, 21–22
fans, British royalty, 81, 84, 162

188

fear, aging, 180–181
fear, boats, 79
fear, illness, 100
financial difficulties, 101, 134–135
first band, 41
first hit song, 71
first musical composition, 27
first song sold, 48, 50
funeral, 186
hobbies, 24, 26
illness, 138, 165–166, 175–177, 183–184
interest in music, 31
international acclaim, 59, 78, 85
interviews, 10, 12
kidnapping plot, 67
leadership of band, 51
marriage, 34
movies, 73, 108, 117, 126, 161–162
music agency, 34
musical collaboration, 48, 70, 73, 118
musical education, 31, 108
musical experimentation, 68
musical inspiration, 45, 56–57, 97–98, 166–167
musical style, 106, 119
plays, 126–129, 149, 163–164
protection, Al Capone, 67
radio broadcasts, 67–68, 135
reception, Newport Jazz Festival, 152–156
reception, England, 81–82, 84
reception, France, 85
reception, Holland, 85
reception, Sweden, 112
reception, Texas, 88
recording, 54, 56, 72–73, 106, 134, 136–137, 142, 149, 152–153, 157
relationship, band members, 70–71, 94–96, 143
relationship, mother, 101
relationship, son, 178, 180–181
relatives, 22
resurgence in popularity, 156–157, 159–160
tour, Africa, 166, 170, 176
tour, Latin America, 171
tours, Cribbean, 161, 166
tours, Europe, 79–85, 96–97, 101–112, 138, 142, 161–162, 166, 170–171, 176
tours, Orient, 166, 171
tours, U.S., 56–57, 76–77, 87–90, 173
tour, World, 165
use of language, 182–183
Washingtonians, 41, 47, 50
White House appearances, 16, 18
youth, 21–34
Ellington, Evie (Beatrice Ellis, longtime companion of Duke Ellington), 11, 148, 183–184, 186
Ellington, James Edward (father of Duke Ellington), 21
death, 102

Ellington, Mercer (son of Duke Ellington), 11, 51–53, 113, 116–117, 177–178, 180, 183
Ellington, Ruth, (sister of Duke Ellington), 10, 22, 113, 116–117, 180, 183
Ellis, Beatrice, *see* Ellington, Evie
Fitzgerald, Ella, 57, 77, 161
Gangsters, 51
Gertler, Gene, 84, *see also* Diamond, Renee and Leslie
Gonsalves, Paul, 18, 95, 146–147, 154–155, 174, 176, 184
Goodman, Benny, 105, 137
Grant, Henry, 31
Greer, Sonny, 40–46, 61, 65, 139, 143–144
Hardwick, Otto "Toby," 40–41, 78, 92, 137
Hodges, Johnny, 57, 95–96, 102, 144, 149, 173–174
Hollywood Club, *see* Kentucky Club
Hurricane Club, 135
"It Don't Mean A Thing If It Ain't Got That Swing," 100, 106
Jazz festivals, 152
Jenkins, Freddy, 65, 68, 92–93
Johnson, Lyndon B., 18
"Jump for Joy," 126–129
Kennedy, John F., 164, 166
Kentucky Club, 50–51, 56
King, Martin Luther, Jr., 164
Logan, Arthur, M.D., 11, 100, 165, 176–177

London Palladium, 79–81
Medal of Freedom, receipt of, 11–12, 16
Metropolitan Opera House, concert, 143
Mills, Irving, 59, 61, 68, 72–73, 78, 125
Modern jazz, 152
"Mood Indigo," 18, 70–72, 97, 100
"My People," 164
National Association for the Advancement of Colored People (NAACP), 30, 143
Nixon, Richard M., 9
Oliver, Joe "King," 60, 64, 136
Perry, "Doc," 32
Practical jokes among band, 90–92
Prince George, 81
Prince of Wales, 81, 84
Racism, 16, 22, 76–77, 85, 88
"Reminiscing in Tempo," 101–102
"Rent" parties, 32–33
Rivalry, band members, 93
Roaring twenties, 59–60
"Royal Ancestry," 161
Savoy Ballroom, 107
Smith, Ada "Bricktop," 47, 78
Smith, Willie "The Lion," 19, 45, 47, 173
Snowden, Elmer, 48, 50
"Soda Fountain Rag," 27
"Solitude," 72–73
Speakeasies, 44
Strayhorn, Billy "Sweetpea," 113–122, 139, 161, 167, 183

"Such Sweet Thunder," 161
Swing, 105
Touring lifestyle, 89, 92–93, *see also* Ellington, Edward Kennedy "Duke," tours, U.S.
Truman, Harry S., 16
Vaudeville, 44–45
Waller, Fats, 40, 46
Washingtonians, 47, 50, 54, 144
  original members, 41
"What Do You Do When The Bed Breaks Down?" 30
White House, 16, 21
William Morris Agency, 125, 135
World's Fair, 1933, 87
World War II, 129

HOLLOWAY HOUSE PUBLISHING CO.

8060 Melrose Ave., Los Angeles, California 90046

- ☐ **NAT TURNER** (ISBN 0-87067-551-6) **$3.95**
- ☐ **PAUL ROBESON** (ISBN 0-87067-552-4) **$3.95**
- ☐ **ELLA FITZGERALD** (ISBN 0-87067-553-2) **$3.95**
- ☐ **MALCOLM X** (ISBN 0-87067-554-0) **$3.95**
- ☐ **JACKIE ROBINSON** (ISBN 0-87067-555-9) **$3.95**
- ☐ **MATTHEW HENSON** (ISBN 0-87067-556-7) **$3.95**
- ☐ **SCOTT JOPLIN** (ISBN 0-87067-557-5) **$3.95**
- ☐ **LOUIS ARMSTRONG** (ISBN 0-87067-558-3) **$3.95**
- ☐ **SOJOURNER TRUTH** (ISBN 0-87067-559-1) **$3.95**
- ☐ **CHESTER HIMES** (ISBN 0-87067-560-5) **$3.95**
- ☐ **BILLIE HOLIDAY** (ISBN 0-87067-561-3) **$3.95**
- ☐ **RICHARD WRIGHT** (ISBN 0-87067-562-1) **$3.95**
- ☐ **ALTHEA GIBSON** (ISBN 0-87067-563-X) **$3.95**
- ☐ **JAMES BALDWIN** (ISBN 0-87067-564-8) **$3.95**
- ☐ **WILMA RUDOLPH** (ISBN 0-87067-565-6) **$3.95**
- ☐ **SIDNEY POITIER** (ISBN 0-87067-566-4) **$3.95**
- ☐ **JESSE OWENS** (ISBN 0-87067-567-2) **$3.95**
- ☐ **MARCUS GARVEY** (ISBN 0-87067-568-0) **$3.95**
- ☐ **JOE LOUIS** (ISBN 0-87067-570-2) **$3.95**
- ☐ **HARRY BELAFONTE** (ISBN 0-87067-571-0) **$3.95**
- ☐ **LENA HORNE** (ISBN 0-87067-572-9) **$3.95**

Gentlemen I enclose $ _____ ☐ cash ☐ check ☐ money order, payment in full for books ordered. I understand that if I am not completely satisfied, I may return my order within 10 days for a complete refund. (Add $1.00 per order to cover postage and handling. CA Residents add 8¼% sales tax 15¢ per book. Please allow 6 weeks for delivery.)

Name _____

Address _____

City _____ State _____ Zip _____